THE BATSFORD BOOK OF HAND AND MACHINE KNITTING

THE BATSFORD BOOK OF HAND AND MACHINE KNITTING

TESSA LORANT

Photography by
Tessa Lorant and
Jeremy Warburg

B T Batsford Ltd London

To my husband, who helped so much

© Tessa Lorant 1980
First published 1980

ISBN 0 7134 3316 7

Filmset in Monophoto Univers by
Servis Filmsetting Ltd, Manchester

Printed in Great Britain by
The Anchor Press Ltd
Tiptree Essex

For the publishers
B T Batsford Ltd
4 Fitzhardinge Street
London W1H 0AH

CONTENTS

ACKNOWLEDGMENT

I would like to thank Aisin (UK) Ltd for information on the Toyota KS 787 machine and for the photographs used in figures 35 and 57; the Bogod Machine Co Ltd for information on the Passap Duomatic 80 machine and for the photograph in figure 45; Barry Bryant Ltd for information on the Superba S-42 machine; the Jones Sewing Machine Co Ltd for information on the Brother KH 830 machine and the photograph used in figure 55; Knitmaster Ltd for information on their machines, for giving me the opportunity to try their electronic KS 500 machine, and for the photographs used in figures 36, 37, 56 and 58; and the Singer Co (UK) Ltd for information on the Singer Memomatic KE 2400 machine and for the photograph in figure 46.

I would also like to thank the International Wool Secretariat for permission to reproduce the Woolmark in figure 62, Diana Shaman for checking the US addresses, and the Chalice Well Trust, Glastonbury, for permission to take photographs at the Chalice Well (plate 5). I am particularly grateful to my son Richard for test knitting the patterns used in this book and for knitting some of the garments illustrated in the colour plates.

Note
The metric and imperial measurements are not exact equivalents, but are convenient sizes in each system.

1 TO KNIT OR NOT TO KNIT

Knitting and crochet are ancient crafts, but this doesn't mean that only the nostalgic practise them. Fresh, open-minded approaches, the invention of new machines, new fibres and new yarns have immensely increased the potential of these crafts. Traditional skills wedded to these modern inventions can produce a remarkable variety of fabrics; these can be shaped or cut, and used to make stylish, warm and, above all, original clothes for anyone – from the top fashion model to the working farmer.

And one needn't stop there; soft furnishings, wall hangings, even pictures worked right into the fabric, can be readily made. This book aims to get you started. It's for those who enjoy yarns and crafted fabric, for the would-be artist who has a feel for colour and form and texture, who would rather create than manufacture, and who would like to use yarns, needles and machines much as a painter uses paints, brushes and support.

Knitting can be enjoyed by everyone – men as well as women, boys as well as girls, the academic and the practical, the beginner and the expert. There's no need for any conflict between knitting by hand or by machine – on the contrary, traditional methods combined with modern technology add richness to both crafts and I'm sure that a good deal more can be done with this combination than by taking up the attitude that machine knitting is not a proper craft, that it's somehow base or mechanical, that a 'real' knitter only knits by hand. On the other hand, I certainly wouldn't substitute machine work for all handwork, or think that the latter is a thing of the past and the effort needed to learn good handwork a waste of time. Crochet, in particular, has always seemed to me a marvellous way to finish hand or machine knitted articles. I shall discuss this more fully in Chapter 2.

The important point is to work in your own way. Though patterns are useful, you'll find you can improve on them almost at once, so don't feel you have to follow 'experts'. Try knitting. Get a friend to show you how to do the first basic, simple steps or start by following the directions in Chapter 2. If you find you enjoy handwork, don't feel bound by rules. Experiment; be adventurous. You'll make some dreadful mistakes, but you'll get some thrilling rewards. If you want to knit, you'll soon find your own way of learning.

There are a lot of practical reasons for knitting, and I'll discuss some of them shortly, under separate headings.

Practical reasons are fine, of course: knitting can make and save money and impress the rest of your family; but they're not the only, and possibly they're not the best reasons. There's nothing to stop you learning to knit because you want to be creative. It's no more a waste of time and money than painting pictures or playing golf or taking photographs. Compared to these activities it's not an expensive pastime, and if you feel you have to produce something practical every time you knit you won't get the creative enjoyment out of it which you should and which I'll show you how you can.

It *is* possible to earn money by knitting, and I discuss this in detail in my *Earning and Saving with a Knitting Machine* (see further reading list). Here I'll just say that I've found marketing knitwear relatively easy. Most people choose their own clothes, and have definite views about it. This means that they'll be interested in looking at knitwear, they'll be delighted to find something original, and glad to pay a little extra so long as they find the garment practical and aesthetically pleasing. I think you can be confident that you'll be able to sell some of your work if you want to, once you've acquired the necessary skill to make it well. It's not, I should add, a particularly easy way to make money, or to make much profit at all. But if you're content to enjoy what you're doing, happy to be paid, in effect, for the machines and tools and materials you use, and to make a little money as well, you won't go far wrong.

People used to hand knit for money. It's a dying craft, because no one will pay enough for the time involved. A few hand knitters remain – in Ireland, for instance. The knitters that do remain often use knitting machines, and I am sure it is machine knitters who will have to evolve ways of preserving, as well as improving on, the traditional craft.

As I've said, it's not too difficult to sell crafted clothes. Machine knits are no exception, and of course it makes economic sense to charge much less for machine knitting because it takes so much less time than knitting by hand. Still, there are one or two things to bear in mind. Don't underprice yourself. You're offering a skill and the use of an expensive piece of equipment. Even if you enjoy machine knitting, ask a realistic price for your work. You're taking work from other people – unduly undercutting them – if you charge too little.

Now I'm going to discuss reasons for choosing these particular crafts. Machine knitting will take up a large part of the discussion, largely because the domestic knitting machine has made this crafted fabric very much faster to produce than hand knitting, crochet or any allied crafts. Sewing by hand or machine will be touched on, though both dress-making and embroidery can only be briefly referred to in this book. A few other techniques will be mentioned where they're relevant, but the main idea is to speed up and extend the range of craftwork by using domestic knitting and sewing machines, and adopting the slower methods primarily for the finishing touches.

Flexibility

Knitwear has become very popular. From the wearer's point of view, one of the differences between knitted and other types of fabric is that of flexibility, or 'give'. The fabric we're mainly concerned with in this book is single knit fabric, easily made by hand or knitting machine. It's constructed by making one yarn loop, called a stitch, then adding more loops, which in turn have yarn pulled in and out of them in various ways with the aid of simple tools such as knitting needles or more sophisticated ones such as knitting machines. Whichever tool is used to produce the fabric, each row of loops retains considerable flexibility; it can be stretched in any direction and will spring back into shape when the tension is released. Figure 1 shows the smooth side of a piece of jersey (see page 8) in three states: stretched sideways to widen and shorten the fabric and the loops; at its normal tension; and stretched lengthways to narrow and lengthen the loops and fabric. The contrasting row shows what happens to a 'course' of knitting in each case.

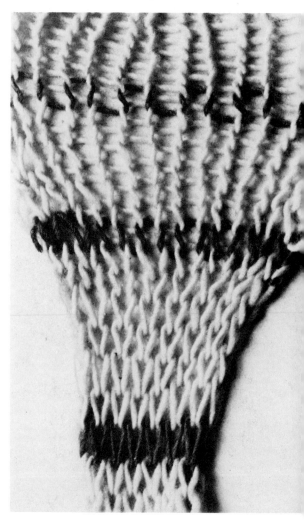

Figure 1 *The flexibility of knitwear: the smooth side of a piece of jersey stretched horizontally to widen it, allowed to find its own tension, and stretched vertically to shorten it in width*

Fabrics produced by other methods, for example weaving or crochet, can have many advantages, but to my mind they have one fundamental flaw: the result isn't sufficiently flexible; the fabric doesn't mould to the body in the way knitted fabric does, and for that reason I prefer knitted fabric as the main material for many of my clothes. I like clothes that move with me, not clothes that tell me how to move.

As Chapter 2 points out, the fact that crocheted fabric is so much less flexible than knitted fabric makes it particularly good for some of the finishing touches in knitwear. Though crochet, too, is made of loops, the stretch is confined to individual loops

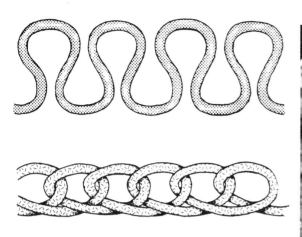

Figure 2 *Comparing flexibilities. From top to bottom: a row of plain knitted loops, a row of crochet chains and a row of woven fabric*

or the spaces between stitches; in ordinary knitting, the stretch is along the whole row. Figure 2 compares a row of woven fabric, a row of knitting and a row of chain stitch crochet.

Warmth

We all know about the energy crisis. Knitted fabric can keep bodies warm; you can turn the central heating down. Since the oil crisis we've cut the oil consumption in our house by half. We've been able to do this mainly because we've used knitwear judiciously. The loose stitches in a knitted fabric trap the air, much as a double window does, and forms a warming layer around the body. Just bear this principle in mind; it's amazing how much lower the background temperature can be if you wear a layer or two of knitted fabric. I'm sure you've heard of thermal underwear. Of course part of the reason for its warmth is the yarn, but knitting any yarn into various patterns creates some warmth. The usual jersey fabric, closely knitted in a fine yarn, makes very good underwear. Some lace patterns are even more effective. They look dainty and delicate, but have quite remarkable warming power. Some young people use this type of commercially available underwear as knitted blouses; the colours could be improved on, but it's a marvellous idea. So there we have our first layer – functional or pretty. For maximum warmth the garment needs to be figure hugging, but for underwear that's no problem. (See figure 3.)

Figure 3 *Punch lace: this figure hugging leotard is made by using the punch lace pattern available on some types of punchcard knitting machine*

I know of only one supplier of thermacrylic yarn for domestic knitters. This is a medium yarn, which is heavier than one might like. (See figure 4.) As a matter of fact you won't lose all that much warmth if you use any, preferably shiny, synthetic yarn; I've found from experience that, knitted fairly tightly and preferably in a rib or tuck stitch pattern, these yarns provide very nearly as much warmth as thermal ones. Shininess is useful, too; it produces a somewhat slippery fabric, and is ideal for wearing under woollen knitwear. Cotton and silk also make excellent underwear, and, if you can tolerate it next to your skin, wool is still unsurpassed for warmth.

Figure 4 *Thermal knitwear: this blouse is made in a 3-ply chlorofibre/acrylic yarn available by mail order*

•**Figure 5** *A sweater knitted in Shetland wool: the leotard in figure 3 can be worn under this*

Using machine washable yarns for the first layer helps to solve the problems associated with laundering knitwear. Some specially treated wools can be washed in a machine – I'll discuss this more fully in Chapter 5.

Sweaters, jumpers, pullovers, jerseys, guernseys: these have been used for warmth for so long they need no introduction from me. They're what I call the second layer, and are best made in a medium to thick yarn. If you choose your underwear carefully, this second layer can have any stylish shape you

fancy; wide sleeves are not as warm as sleeves gathered at the wrist, but with the right underwear you don't need to worry about that. Some stitch patterns take more yarn, but the extra thickness created by this gives much greater warmth. Fairisle – that is two or more colour knitting – considerably increases the warmth because of the floats, the loose strands of yarn carried along the back of the fabric when knitting with several colours. Dresses, skirts and trousers may form this layer. Knitting these requires extra thought: they must have good 'hang' as well as warmth, and I'll discuss this more fully later. Here I'm trying to show how to 'layer' the warmth. Figure 5 shows a sweater worn over the leotard shown in figure 3.

Then there are the various thick knits, the over jumpers and cardigans, jackets and ponchos. Usually made in bulky yarns they're often quick to hand knit. This, I think, is the reason for their popularity. Personally I find knits made of these very thick yarns heavy to wear, difficult to wash, and not worth their weight in warmth. I do use the bulky yarns, but woven into a thinner knitted fabric rather than used in actual knitting. Again, I shall discuss this at some length in Chapter 6. Whatever method they're made by, these thick knits are useful for driving, and for travelling generally; they're adequately flexible and very warm except in windy situations. In these they're much less use, though a thin, waterproofed nylon anorak or stormcoat will deal with wind and rain. Figure 6 shows a knitwoven jacket over the sweater shown in figure 5.

Costs

There's no quick or easy answer to the question of whether you save on costs by knitting for yourself. I think we should deal with this in some detail. First of all I'll break down the items that go to make up the cost. Then I'll give three examples of the types of garments most commonly bought, how much each costs to produce, and the conclusions that I've drawn from this for my purposes. You may well come to different conclusions for your own purposes.

Tools You have to have some sort of tool to knit or crochet with. If you intend to do handwork, the cost of these tools will be negligible in relation to the time they last.

The high investment cost comes when you buy a knitting machine. If I concentrate on a single bed automatic punchcard domestic knitting machine and break down the costs of using one of these, you'll be able to compare that with using any other, cheaper or more expensive one. For instance, if you buy a second-hand machine for half the price of a new automatic punchcard machine, you halve the costs.

An automatic punchcard machine will cost about £250 ($500), roughly the same as an expensive automatic camera. Some will be a little more, some a little less, and some suppliers give a greater discount than others. Ignoring other factors for the moment, I think it's fair to give a new machine a life of about

Figure 6 *A knitwoven jacket: this can form the third layer over the leotard and the sweater. The ribbed sweater collar repeats one of the yarns used in the jacket to provide a coordinated look*

ten years. We could calculate that the machine will cost £25 ($50) a year, on average. How much it costs for each garment obviously depends on how many you make. If you make only five garments a year, the cost of using the machine will be £5 ($10) for each one. On the other hand, if you make a hundred, the machine cost will be only 25p (50c) for each one. I can't put a price on your use of your machine, so, in my costing, I've put the price of paying someone else to do the work; you can always adjust this figure in your own case. If you want to use your machine purely for art or pleasure, with no intention of saving money, I think it's excellent value.

Yarns The next item to consider is the yarn; obviously you can't produce anything without it. The cost of yarn varies a great deal. Yarn bought on the cone from a mail order supplier is very much cheaper and more convenient than yarn bought from the High Street yarn shop. If you go straight to the mills, it's cheaper still. To get really good bargains you need to order in bulk, perhaps 5 kg (11 lbs) of yarn at a time. This sounds a great deal but it's quickly knitted up. You can also buy balled yarns by mail order; these are cheaper than they would be in the High Street, but not such outstanding bargains. There's a list of suppliers at the end of the book.

Labour The most difficult part to assess, in some ways, is the labour cost. You might well say it doesn't cost anything because you're using leisure time. I don't think this is strictly accurate. It's still useful to think in terms of what your time is worth, because it does cost you something to use it in this way. You might spend it growing vegetables or baking bread or playing with the children. If you spend it knitting by hand while chatting or watching TV, you're not using very much extra time or energy, though you are using some. If you're knitting by machine, you're using a fair amount of energy, though for a shorter time. So there is a price on your time. Only you can decide what that price is.

For costing garments, it might be best to think of it another way.

What is the least it would cost to employ someone else to do machine knitting? I think you'd hardly expect to pay less than £1 ($2) an hour and this is an easy amount to think about. Handwork might well be thought of as costing 50p ($1) an hour. So for a reasonable assessment of the value of machine knitted articles you need to add £1 ($2) for every hour spent knitting on your machine, £1 ($2) for every hour spent sewing up on an electric sewing machine, and 50p ($1) for every hour spent sewing up or finishing by hand.

Now we can consider the value of crafting. Take that very common garment, the slim fitting polo neck jumper manufactured in a synthetic yarn. I don't think you'd consider hand knitting this. The yarn used is quite fine and it would take a long time. The work involved in machine knitting the garment, though not at all difficult, is time-consuming and

rather dull. You'll want to use the finest yarn possible on your machine. That means a large number of rows to the centimetre or inch, which in turn means sliding the carriage to and fro a great many times. Even if the garment isn't shaped as you knit, and cut and sew methods reduce actual knitting time considerably, it will still take about three hours to knit and cut out. Sewing up on a sewing machine will probably take another hour. The total time spent will be around four hours. For something you can buy so easily and so inexpensively, this hardly seems worthwhile.

Now we could consider an ordinary, plain wool jumper. Let's assume it takes about four hours to knit and sew up a simple jumper which has the minimum of shaping. I'm allowing for a little handwork in the finishing process. Are you getting good value? I think you are. We're comparing this jumper with one you might buy at a chain store. These jumpers will have been made in a cheap wool; it will be pure wool if the label says so, but there are many qualities of wool. It will be skimpy in length, the ribbing won't be very elastic, and if a hole appears you won't have the darning wool handy. These commercially made jumpers don't last long because the wool used breaks so easily. This means you soon get holes. Your own jumper will have the quality of the wool you've chosen to pay for, and the time spent will be the same, whatever quality you choose. It will be a good length and the ribbing or other welts sturdy and elastic. I think it worthwhile to make all my own jumpers, and the family's.

Now let's consider the thick knits. The yarns you find most readily in the local shops are mixtures of various fibres. There's nothing wrong with them, in fact there's a marvellous choice. They're designed especially for fast hand knitting, and for that they work very well. The trouble is that thick knits take a large amount of yarn and if you knit a jacket, say, you have a pretty expensive garment. I use these thick yarns for knitweaving on my machine. This is one of the patterns some knitting machines do very well and, though it's not completely automatic, it's still quite quick to do. Chapter 6 deals in some detail with this method of using a knitting machine, but here I'd just like to point out that you can get all the warmth of the thick yarn at a fraction of the cost. Knitweave really means that you are getting a medium-weight knitted fabric with thick yarn woven into that fabric as a base. So the cost of a garment made in this way will be the cost of a medium-weight garment together with the cost of the thick weaving yarn.

Using the yarn for weaving rather than knitting means you use between one-third and one-half of the thick yarn. The machine knitting time will be longer than for ordinary knitting. I find it takes four to five hours to knitweave a jacket, and two to three hours to finish it by sewing machine and by hand. Jackets made in this way not only compare favourably with bought ones on cost, they're also simple to turn into original creations because of the different ways the two yarns can be combined.

For more ambitious garments you can't lose by making your own – they would only be available commercially from boutiques stocking designer clothes. The cost of these would be far higher than producing your own.

Savings

You can make other savings. It's not just a question of calculating the cost of the materials and labour. You can certainly save by buying yarn economically and ignoring the cost of your time. You can also save a great deal by having coordinated clothes, often called mix and match clothes. This means that you decide on a basic colour scheme, then build your wardrobe round that. When you hand knit, crochet or machine knit many of your clothes, you can use related colours, blend the colour of one piece into a trimming of another, and generally make everything 'go' with everything else. Making reversible clothes, like the jacket in Pattern 3, is a useful option. You can make one garment do a lot of work, and by taking fewer clothes you will save space and weight when packing for your holidays, for instance.

Another big saving is in children's clothes. To give you just one example on how worthwhile savings in money and time can be made, just imagine lengthening a toddler's jumper at the cuff of the sleeve and at the waist. Children tend to grow longer rather than wider for a year or two at a time, so a toddler's jumper can be made reasonably wide in the first place. Then, as soon as it shows signs of getting too short, you need only undo or take off the waist welt, add a section of plain or patterned knitting, and knit or graft the welt on again. Coloured patterns make use of spare yarn and hide slight colour changes in the original yarn used.

You can also save by making rather than buying presents. You will probably buy yarn in bulk. Those part-used cones can make original, colourful and warm scarf and hat sets. Smaller amounts of left over yarn can be used for patchwork blankets, bed-spreads, cushion covers or even rugs. Many small items are often expensive in the shops yet quick to make. People will also very much enjoy being given 'real' presents; something you've taken the trouble to make especially for them.

Fit

You may be stock size and have no problems fitting into bought clothing. In any case, knitwear is flexible, so sizing is not as vital as in woven fabric. However, there are still a few difficulties. The greatest of these is length. Manufacturers save as much yarn as they can to keep their prices low. This always means that mass produced knitwear is a bit on the skimpy side. If you're small, you can buy a larger size. If you're a tall woman, you can buy a man's jumper for the extra length. But if you're a tall man you're in trouble. Your arms will be longer than average, so will your trunk, and buying a larger size won't help much because fat men are often short, and the extra width only partly makes up for the lack of length.

You may be extra wide as well as extra long, in which case I don't need to tell you how much easier life will be if you make your own knitwear. Extra large sizes are always more expensive, not only because they use more material, but also because the manufacturer's run isn't long enough to allow for much cost cutting.

Choice

The question of size leads to the question of choice. There really is a lot of choice if you're stock size. Even so, there's a curious sameness about the mass produced article, presumably because methods of production are so similar. For something different you have to pay a much higher price.

For something different at a reasonable price you will need to make your own garments. Even if you use a commercial pattern, you're free to select the colour and the yarn, so long as you learn how to adapt your own choice of yarn to the pattern you're using. Once you're used to making your own things you'll find it easy to adapt commercial patterns, even to make patterns of your own.

It's creating your own fabric which makes for the greatest differences. There's an enormous choice of yarns in this country, and the different combinations are enough to satisfy almost anyone. If you want to increase your range still further you can buy undyed or light-coloured yarn and dye it yourself. This should give you subtle shades which no one can copy exactly – particularly if you use vegetable dyes.

New shapes

Often the shape you want is shown in the latest fashion magazines, but the local boutique can't get it from the manufacturers yet. All you have to do is work the pattern out for yourself. You won't want to make a slavish copy of the photograph because that's someone else's idea, and anyway you may well improve on it, but if waistcoats are 'in' you might like one right away, and if dirndl skirts are 'in' you can make one quite easily yourself.

Modern fashion uses simple shapes, so all you need to do is to think which of these you'd like and combine them in the latest look.

But apart from the new shapes in the fashions you see around you, what about the shapes you'd like for yourself and don't often see? Have you ever asked yourself, 'Why don't they make extra wide collars to set off my hairstyle?' There must be hundreds of things like that which you'd like to see in shop clothes but haven't come across. That's another good reason for making at any rate some of your own things. For example, I don't like the way fine knitted lace blouses ride up under trousers or skirts, so I shape them into leotards, the kind that ballet dancers wear. (See figure 3.)

Know how

There's a useful spin-off in knowing how clothes are put together. You'll soon find that you know how to look at the finish, quality and general value of bought garments in a much more professional way. Some things are just not worth making, however quick you are, however skilled. Slim fit polo-necked jumpers and knitted underwear are probably best bought, because industrial machines can handle finer yarn than domestic machines, and because the saving is not large enough to make the effort of manufacturing them yourself worthwhile. It depends not only on how you value your time, but on what you like to do with it.

Pleasure

And now for perhaps the most important reason for doing your own crafting, including knitting: it will give you a great deal of pleasure. As your skill improves and you extend your knowledge from simple knitting and crochet to advanced work and knitting machines, then to combinations of all kinds of needlework, you'll get that thrill and that wonderful sense of satisfaction that comes from being creative. It's no longer just a question of saving money, or of saving or passing time. That you can do, but you don't have to. You may borrow other people's ideas and incorporate them in your own work, but you won't be content to stay a follower of other people's fashions, methods, materials. You'll invent and create, solve problems, even use mistakes to get new slants on your work. You need never be at a loss for something to make, for something satisfying to do.

2 HAND KNITTING AND CROCHET

Ways of needlecrafting

There are several ways of knitting by hand, several ways of crocheting, and several machines to use for machine knitting. There are allied crafts like macramé and quilting, weaving and tatting. You can learn embroidery and sewing, by machine or by hand. You can learn to make lace, to candlewick, to do pulled thread work . . . The list of things you can make with yarn, fabric and the appropriate tools is extensive.

If you have the urge to create, you'll try many of these methods because they'll increase your range. It's not so much a matter of learning to knit or crochet; it's a matter of being glad to be shown methods other people have evolved, and – using the knowledge they've made available – of evolving methods of one's own, and passing these on in turn.

Hand knitting

I'm sure you already know what hand knitting is and that it's done with needles and yarn. A number of yarn loops, called stitches, are put on one needle, another is used to work them. It's really a very simple process; you don't have to have sophisticated equipment – given two knitting needles and a reasonable amount of yarn you can make a splendid fabric. However, though the end result is similar, there are several ways of producing it. The yarn can be threaded through the right or left hand fingers, and the stitch-forming needle is held in the right or left hand, depending on whether the knitter is right or left handed. The second needle is held in the other hand.

The method chosen matters because the speed of knitting, the evenness of the stitches and the

Figure 7 *One method of holding and tensioning the yarn for hand knitting*

Figure 8 *Casting on*

pleasure in doing the work are much affected by it. Describing more than one method of forming stitches is outside the scope of this book, but the reading list gives the titles of some specialist books on hand knitting stitch patterns and methods.

English method

I have chosen to describe this method because I find it produces the most even stitches, though it's slower than other methods. Once you've acquired the basic technique, you can always change to another method which may suit you better.

The yarn is held in the right hand, wound once round the little finger, passing under the two middle fingers, and over the index finger. The right hand needle is used to make stitches from the loops held on the left hand needle. (See figure 7.)

Casting on One method of starting to knit, or casting on, is to make a slip knot and loop it over the left hand needle. Hold the yarn at the back. Put the point of the right hand needle through the front to the back of the loop, pass the yarn round the needle and draw through a new loop. Slip this new loop onto the left hand needle to form a new stitch.

Continue until the required number of stitches are on the left hand needle. (See figure 8.)

Knitting proper can now be started. There are two stitches, called *plain* or *knit*, and *purl*. Combinations of these two basic stitches form the stitch patterns.

Plain or knit stitch The plain or knit stitch is made by holding the yarn at the back of the work. Put the right hand needle through the first stitch or loop on the left hand needle from the front to the back, pass the yarn round and slip through a new loop. Leave this on the right hand needle, dropping the loop from the left hand needle and pulling the yarn to get the correct tension. The new plain stitch is on the right hand needle. (See figure 9.)

Purl stitch The purl stitch is made by putting the yarn to the front of the work. Put the right hand needle through the first loop on the left hand needle from the back to the front, loop the yarn over it, and pull back a loop while slipping the original loop from the left hand needle, pulling the yarn to get the correct tension. The new purl stitch is on the right hand needle. (See figure 10.)

In order to shape a garment while knitting, it's necessary to increase and decrease stitches.

16

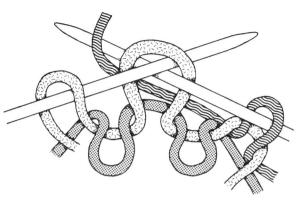

Figure 9 *Making a knit stitch*

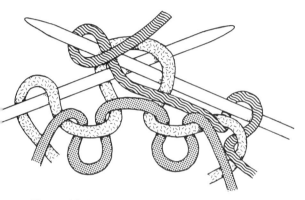

Figure 10 *Making a purl stitch*

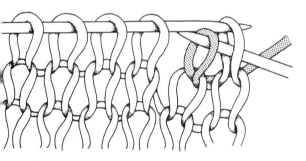

Figure 11 *Casting off*

Increase To increase one stitch, knit into the next stitch on the left hand needle and, without dropping it from the left hand needle, bring the yarn to the front of the work and purl into the same stitch. There will be an extra stitch on the right hand needle.

Decrease The simplest way to decrease is to put the right hand needle through two stitches on the left hand needle and knit or purl them off together.

There are many different methods of increasing and decreasing; specialist stitch pattern books usually give a good selection, and garment patterns often specify a particular method.

Selvedge You can choose how your knitted edge will look; for the beginner, knitting the first and last stitch of every row, regardless of the stitch pattern, makes an excellent and easy edge. There are many variations.

Casting off In order to end up with a fabric without open loops, a method has to be devised to finish it. The simplest is to knit two stitches onto the right hand needle; then, with the point of the left hand needle, pull the first over the second stitch on the right hand needle, leaving only one stitch. Now knit another stitch, and repeat the process. (See figure 11.) Casting off can be done knitways or purlways, and should be done according to the pattern being worked. The cast off row will not have the same flexibility as the rest of the knitting. Using a larger needle for casting off makes sure this finish is not too tight. After the casting off is complete, cut the yarn and pull it through the last loop.

Held stitches Where casting off is carried out in a series of steps, as at a shoulder, the stitches can be 'held' on the needle without being worked, then cast off along the whole row at the end of the shaping. To avoid a hole, slip the first stitch after turning instead of working it.

Ways of hand knitting

One method of carrying out all the basic movements for hand knitting has been described. Two needles are used to make each stitch, but a number of needles may be used for the work. The following is a brief review of the more usual methods.

Two needle knitting The commonest method of knitting is to use two needles only, producing a flat piece of work by knitting backwards and forwards along rows, and using needles with knobs at one end and points at the other. The knobs stop the stitches coming off the needles by mistake, the points are used to pull the yarn through the loops or stitches. There is a back and front to the work, though some fabric looks the same on both sides. The work is turned at the end of each row, the working needle becoming the needle which holds the stitches.

Figure 12 *Twin pins, or circular needles, being used to knit an armhole facing*

Circular knitting Four or more needles, pointed at both ends, can be used to make a piece of tubing with no seams. The same effect can be produced by using 'twin pins', two pointed needle ends connected by a flexible nylon wire, which comes in short lengths for small numbers of stitches and longer lengths for larger numbers of stitches. The twin pins are easy to knit with because there are no 'joins' to be considered where you go from one needle to another. On the other hand, you have to have enough stitches to be able to get round the round. Also, the shortness of the needle ends makes it strange to knit in this way at first. (See figure 12.)

Maxi knitting Some very large knitting needles are available for maxi knitting. These are made of a light or hollow material and are often used with several ends of yarn at a time, sometimes as many as six. Finished articles can be produced very quickly. I've used this method and hand knitted a dress in six hours. The results look very pleasing at first, especially in a good stitch pattern, but the weight of the yarn tends to pull a large garment out of shape, either when it's being worn or when it's being washed. However, it's a quick way to hand knit. Figure 13 shows a piece of maxi knitting and the needles used to make it.

Some people even attempt 'broomstick' knitting. Here needles actually shaped from broomhandles are used to knit up strips of fabric. It's quick and cheap to produce floor-coverings and wall-hangings in this way.

Cable knitting An extra needle, called a *cable needle*, is used to work cable knitting. This is a short needle with points at both ends, but any needle pointed at both ends can be used. A number of stitches is slipped from the left hand needle to the cable needle and held out of the way while the same number of stitches, again from the left hand needle, is worked. (See figure 14.) The group on the cable needle is then brought back to be worked off and the cable needle is put aside until it's needed again. This group can be put to the front or the back of the work, creating different 'cables' or 'plaits'. You've probably seen cables on cricket jumpers, where they are traditionally used.

Figure 13 *A piece of maxi knitting produced by using 5 strands of double knitting yarn and knitting with 25 mm (1 in.) needles*

Knitting a hem An effective way to finish many garments is to make a knitted hem. This is easily done by knitting the depth of the hem required on a tighter tension than the main fabric. Knitting a distinctive turning row to distinguish it from the rest of the pattern can be helpful. Now change to the main tension and knit the second depth of hem. The fabric can be folded back on the turning line, and the hem knitted in by picking up each cast on stitch with the left hand needle and knitting it off together with the corresponding stitch on the right hand needle. Alternatively it can be sewn on later. Plate 1 (facing p. 72) shows a garment with a knitted hem.

A hem can be added to a finished piece of work by picking up the cast on stitches, knitting the depth of the desired hem and sewing the open loops to the corresponding stitches on one side of the work.

Stitch patterns

There are a great many stitch patterns, from delicate filet lace to chunky bobble fabric, from picot knitting to fur fabric stitches. You can invent your own stitches as well as your own designs. One two-needle method of making some of these stitches is given here, but for different methods and for variety it's necessary to consult books especially written on this topic.

Stocking stitch The basic knitted fabric is called *stocking stitch* or *jersey*. It's a fabric with smooth knit stitches on one side, and the rougher purl stitches on the other, called *reverse stocking stitch* or *purl stitch*. In two needle knitting it's produced by knitting one row plain, one row purl and alternating the rows in this way. In circular knitting it's produced by knitting plain all the time. Figure 15 shows a single ridge, made by knitting a section of stocking stitch followed by a section of reversed stocking stitch.

Ridge stitch The best known ridge stitch is *garter stitch*, which is the simplest of all two needle hand knitting stitches. Every stitch on every row is knitted; or, if you prefer purling, every stitch on every row is purled. The fabric will have ridges running horizontally, looks the same on both sides, and is firmer than

Figure 14 *Making a cable: the lower cable is twisted from left to right, the upper one from right to left*

jersey; firm enough to use for maxi knitting, where jersey could be too loose. The ridge pattern can be varied by arranging to have the order of the rows knitted in different ways. One example would be a six row pattern: knit the first, third, fourth and sixth rows, and purl the second and fifth. This will give fairly thick ridges. (See figures 15 and 17.)

Rib stitch Rib stitch is made by knitting plain and purl stitches in a pre-determined pattern in a row, and then knitting the next row in such a way that the plain stitches are purled and the purl stitches are knitted plain. This produces vertical bands of jersey alternated with purl stitch, which look like, and are called, ribs. There are all kinds of rib stitches, fancy and plain, made by alternating knit and purl stitches in various ways, sometimes twisting the stitches for

special effects. Many of the simple rib fabrics are particularly elastic, and, if the ribs are of equal width, similar on both sides. *Single rib* is made by knitting one plain, one purl on each row along the row; *double rib* by knitting two plain, two purl on each row along the row. (See figure 16.)

Seed stitch Instead of knitting ribs, it's easy to purl some of the previous row's purl stitches and knit some of the previous row's knit stitches. In this way a number of 'seed' stitches can be formed, because the chosen purled stitches are shown off as a small button by a ring of plain jersey fabric. The best known form is *moss stitch*, using a knit one, purl one combination. This fabric looks the same on both sides and is popular for garment edges. (See figure 16.)

Drop stitch Drop stitch or *spider stitch* is a simple but effective pattern, having the appearance of lace but requiring very little trouble. It can be made by winding the yarn round the needle several times after knitting each stitch. An example would be to knit each stitch, wind the yarn two or three times round the needle, then knit the next stitch, all along the drop stitch row, ending by knitting a stitch. On the following row, purl the stitches, allowing the extra loops to drop. A band of ordinary jersey fabric between the drop rows heightens the effect, but other stitch patterns can be used. Figure 17 shows a drop stitch between two sections of garter stitch.

Loop stitch Loops can be made between the knitted stitches, and these held in place by knitting through them on the following row. Though slow to work, loop stitch can add contrast and unusual textures to garments; used on collars and cuffs only, for instance, the fabric shows up almost like a fur finish. One simple example is made by knitting the edge stitch, putting the right hand needle into the first stitch of the left hand needle, winding the yarn round this and round the index finger of the left

hand two or three times, then knitting *all* the loops through the stitch in the usual way. There will be several loops on the right hand needle for each stitch worked. This is done on every stitch of the row except the last one. On the return row, every group of two or three loops is knitted as one stitch, which anchors the loops. Several rows of a simple stitch pattern are knitted between the looped rows, depending on the effect wanted. (See figure 18.)

Lace stitch Openwork fabric, giving a lacy look, can be made by 'losing' stitches in one part of a row, and 'making' stitches in the same row or the following row. A simple example would be to knit the first five stitches, put the yarn round the needle once, knit two stitches together, and repeat this all across the row. Purl the next row, treating the yarn round the needle as a stitch. This will form a hole, with six stitches between it and the next hole. If the pattern is shifted one stitch along, a slanting set of holes is formed. Figure 19 shows a simple lace zigzag with a three-stitch bobble set between. All kinds of shapes can be delineated by the holes, from simple geometric shapes to complicated flower and leaf patterns.

Figure 15 *The two sides of stocking stitch, or jersey, fabric*

Bobble stitch Bobbles can be formed by knitting several times into the same stitch. For a three-stitch bobble, insert the right hand needle into the next stitch on the left hand needle as if to knit it, pass the yarn over the needle and bring out a loop. Take the back of this loop onto the left hand needle and knit that stitch onto the right hand needle. Now put the right hand needle through the original stitch, which is still on the left hand needle, and repeat these three steps two more times. Slip the stitch off the left hand needle. There will now be a group of three stitches on the right hand needle. With the tip of the left hand needle, bring the last two of the group of stitches over the first one on the right hand needle, leaving one stitch. There will be a bobble under that stitch. To make the bobble even more pronounced, knit back and forth on the new group of stitches on the right hand needle for two or three rows, then finish as before. (See figure 19.)

Figure 16 *From top to bottom: single rib, moss stitch and double rib* (left)

Figure 17 *Drop, or spider stitch, between two sections of garter stitch*

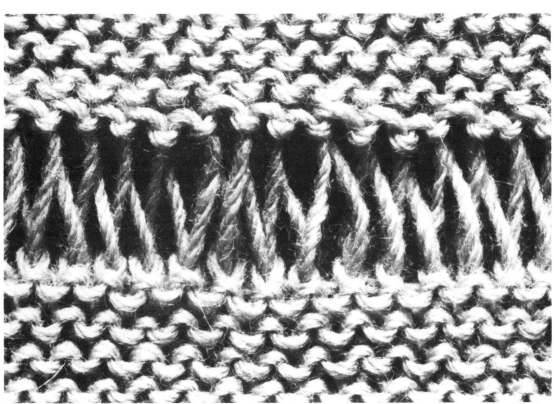

Figure 18 *Loop stitch, here made by knitting one row between two rows of loop stitch, then two rows between the next two sets of loop stitch rows* (above)

Figure 19 *Knitted lace and bobble stitch: a zigzag row of holes creates a lacy fabric. The three-stitch bobble shows up well on the smooth side of jersey.* (below)

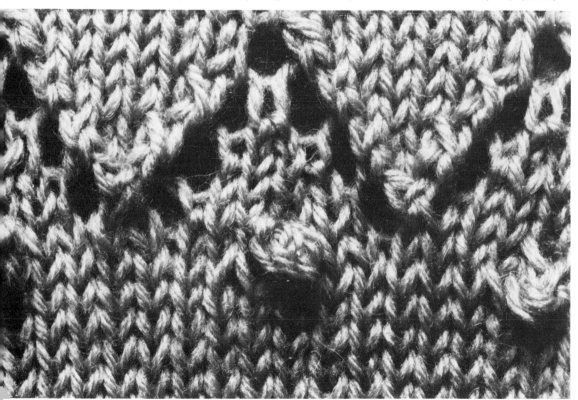

Figure 20 *Slip stitch: the floats outline the pattern on the smooth side of jersey in this particular case* (above)

Figure 21 *Fabric knitted on the bias: the direction is accentuated by the slanting floats on the purl side of a vertical stripe pattern, here folded to make a collar* (below)

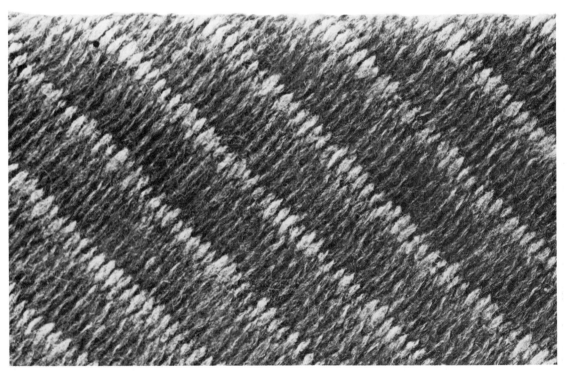

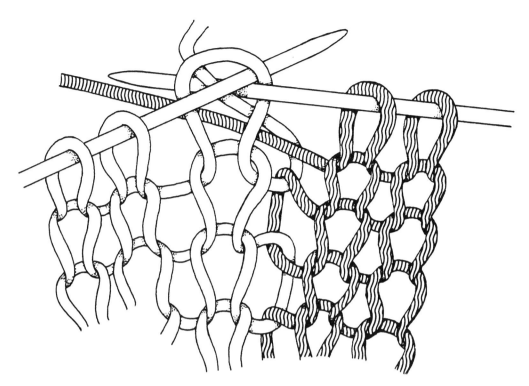

Figure 22 *How to twist two differently coloured yarns at the back of a jersey fabric while working a knit row*

Slip stitch Transferring stitches from the left hand needle to the right hand one without knitting is called slip stitch. This can be done knitways or purlways. By carrying the yarn in front of, or at the back of, the knitting, interesting woven-look fabrics can be made. The 'floats' are used to outline the pattern. (See figure 20).

Bias knitting Bias knitting isn't usually necessary, as knitted fabric is already so flexible. However, it's simple to do and can make some unusual and effective fabrics. Instead of working rows without shaping, increase in the first stitch of the row, work to the last two stitches, then work two together. For a jersey fabric, the shaped row is knitted, the next row purled without shaping or vice versa, and the work continued in this way. The method can be adapted to other stitch patterns. (See figure 21.)

Working with two or more different coloured yarns in a single row gives well-known and popular patterns.

Jacquard Using several colours in one row, with patterns of bold, solid colour, is called Jacquard knitting. 'Argyle' socks are one example. These solid blocks are generally worked in jersey, but other stitch patterns can be used. Only one yarn is being used to make the stitches, the rest are held along the back of the work as 'floats'. Some simple system has to be devised for coping with strands covering more than two or three stitches. One way is to wind small amounts of the different coloured yarns onto cardboard holders and to use several holders to knit sections of solid pattern along the row, twisting the two yarns between any two sections to avoid a hole. Figure 22 shows how to twist the yarns. Patchwork knitting is often done in this way.

Fairisle Fairisle is a jersey fabric knitted by using yarns of different colours in the same knitted row, but in diffused rather than bold colour patches. (See plates 1 and 4 facing pp 72, 73 and figure 75.) The strands not in use are carried at the back of the work, as floats, and must not be drawn too tightly, or the elasticity of the fabric is lost. If the float is very long it is woven into the wrong side of the work by knitting over and under it as the stitches are worked off. Figure 23 shows a float woven in as a knit row is being worked. Traditional fairisle patterns are often made in small repeat patterns – avoiding the problem of long floats – and generally with only two colours to a row, but several colours to the garment. Scandinavian snowflake and general all-over designs are worked on the same principle, though there may be long floats.

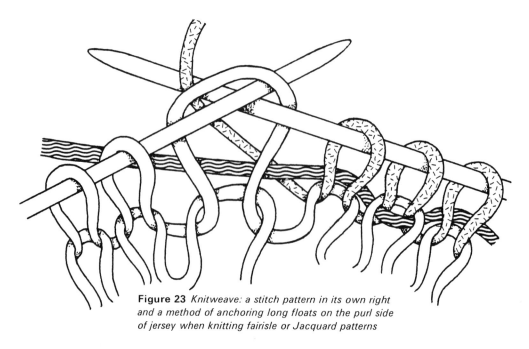

Figure 23 *Knitweave: a stitch pattern in its own right and a method of anchoring long floats on the purl side of jersey when knitting fairisle or Jacquard patterns*

Figure 24 *The smooth side of jersey used as a base for needle weaving a pattern in bulky yarn*

Figure 25 *Making a crochet chain*

Knitweave An interesting fabric can be made by combining knitting and weaving. While the main yarn is being knitted in a jersey or lace stitch, a second, usually much bulkier yarn, is woven in and out of the stitches on each row using the method already described to anchor long floats in multi-colour knitting. However, the floats are deliberately varied in length to create patterns of their own. The weaving yarn is kept on the purl side of the fabric, and woven in simple patterns of one, two or three stitch floats at a time. This is the side which forms the right side in most cases, though interesting reversible fabrics are produced by combining weaving with a lace stitch.

Jersey can also be used like the canvas for a tapestry. Figure 24 shows a bulky yarn needle woven into the smooth side of stocking stitch after the fabric has been knitted.

Crochet

There are several different ways of crocheting, but the method which gives such useful finishing touches for knitted fabrics is called short hook crochet. The simplest and probably the quickest way to finish some edges of a knitted fabric, whether made by hand or machine, is to crochet onto them directly. I haven't timed it but I think it might well take just as long to make a decorative machine edging on a shaped curve as to crochet an edging; but even if it's slightly quicker to machine, you can extend your range considerably by learning to crochet.

Short hook crochet

As with knitting, the basis of short hook crochet is a loop or knot. Instead of a long, pointed needle, a short needle with a hook at one end is used to pull a new loop of yarn through the loops or fabric already made. There will only be a very few stitches on the hook at any one time. The fabric is usually turned at the end of a row, though crocheting in the round can be very effectively used for curved shapes. The two sides of the fabric look similar for the basic stitches.

Casting on It is only necessary to make one slip knot to cast on.

Chain stitch The yarn is held in the left hand, wound once round the little finger, brought under the two middle fingers, then looped over the index finger. The hook is held in the right hand and is used to pull a new loop of yarn through the first loop, making a new stitch. Holding the work between the middle finger and thumb of the left hand, continue to pull new loops through until the required number has been made. This produces a chain of crochet loops. Figure 25 shows a chain of crochet being

27

made. The chain is used as the basic row of a piece of crochet, but crochet stitches can be worked onto any fabric; knitted fabric makes a good base. The basic crochet stitches are all easy to do and involve two actions: putting the yarn round the hook to make extra loops, and pulling the yarn through the fabric or chain already made and then through the loops on the hook. The different stitches are variations of these actions. (See figures 26 and 27.)

Single crochet or slip stitch Put the hook into the stitch to its left, catch the yarn with the hook and draw it through both loops to make a single crochet or slip stitch.

Double crochet (US single crochet) Put the hook into the stitch to its left, catch the yarn and draw it through. There are now two loops on the hook. Catch the yarn again and draw it through both the loops to make a double crochet stitch.

Half treble (US half double crochet) Put the yarn round the hook, then put the hook into the stitch to its left and draw through the yarn. There are now three loops on the hook. Draw the yarn through all three loops to form a half treble stitch, as illustrated in figure 27. When working with crochet already made, you can put the yarn through one or two loops of the chain part of the previous stitch on the left; either method is useful, but the effect is different.

Treble (US double crochet) Put the yarn round the hook, and then put the hook into the stitch to its left and draw through the yarn. There are now three loops on the hook. Draw the yarn through two loops, then through the two remaining loops to form a treble stitch. Deeper stitches can be made by putting the yarn round the hook several times before beginning to crochet off the loops two at a time.

Casting off is simply done by cutting the yarn and pulling it through the last loop.

Increasing Simple increases are worked by crocheting twice into the same stitch.

Decreasing Simple decreases are worked by missing one stitch out. For the deeper stitches, work the first stitch to the last two loops; now work the next stitch, pulling the yarn through the last *three* loops together. This method will avoid an unsightly hole.

Figure 26 *From bottom to top: chain crochet, slip stitch, double crochet, half treble, treble, double treble, triple treble and a picot stitch*

Figure 27 *Making a half treble stitch*

Turning A certain number of chain stitches are added at the end of each row in order to turn the work and start the next row. Make one turning chain for double crochet, two for half treble, three for treble and so on for the deeper stitches. The last chain of the previous row's turning chain is used as the base for the last stitch of the row being worked. (See figure 26.)

Stitch patterns

Filet crochet Because it's so easy to make deep stitches in crochet it's easy to leave spaces producing filet crochet to use as lace or buttonholes. To make a space you merely crochet one of the stitches you've chosen as your basic stitch, leave out the next stitch or stitches by making chains to give length without depth, and then again make a stitch or stitches. You can leave out any number of stitches as you please, producing a lattice work, provided there is enough basic fabric. (See figure 28.)

Figure 28 *Filet crochet: here some of the holes are used as casing for a cord*

Woven crochet The basic fabrics or the lattice fabric can be used like the canvas for a tapestry. Woven crochet can be made using contrasting yarns or long, thin strands of ribbon, leather or other suitable fillers. These can be threaded in and out of the fabrics in various ways to give fascinating and individual results. (See figure 28.)

Cluster stitches Crocheting into the same stitch several times to make cluster stitches is easy. Shell stitches are particularly simple to make; the principle is to crochet a number of the tall stitches into one stitch, then leave spaces on either side, attaching these stitches to the fabric with a slip stitch. The number of stitches, depth and spaces on either side can be varied to suit the size of shell wanted: a simple example would be to make one slip stitch, skip two stitches, crochet five half trebles into the next stitch, skip two stitches and again anchor the shell with a slip stitch. (See plate 6 facing p. 96.)

Picot stitch Another simple but adaptable stitch is made by slip stitching or double crocheting into the fabric, making several chain stitches, double crocheting into the first chain, slip stitching or double crocheting into one or more stitches and then repeating the doubled back chain. Again the size of the chain and the stitches slipped or double crocheted in between can be varied. (See figure 26.)

Advantages of handwork

There's no reason why you shouldn't concentrate on handwork and forget all about the new machines.

In fact there are several reasons why you might prefer to hand knit or crochet. One I've already mentioned: there's no large initial outlay. Another is that you can hand knit or crochet almost anywhere – in bed, travelling, watching TV, talking to friends . . . Also, you don't need a special place, a special light, or much storage space. You can use any yarn, needle or hook size. All the traditional stitch patterns can be worked, any width can be knitted or crocheted, though weight and needle length will impose certain limits. Undoubtedly patterning is more versatile, less mechanical and more adaptable for unplanned design in yarns, stitch patterns and colours. You may not mind the work taking longer. In these days of extra leisure you might even welcome it.

However, I think eventually you'll consider a knitting machine. As I've said before, some people consider knitting by machine not quite a proper craft. They forget that looms are used for weaving and that, however simple needles may be, they are tools. A knitting machine is a rather more complicated sort of tool, but it is just a tool; it can't do anything by itself. The quality of the craft produced by it still depends on the person who's doing the crafting.

Proverbially, every advantage has its disadvantage, every loss its gain. The trick is to turn the loss of hand craft into the gain of machine craft.

So do read the next chapter; and find out what's available in knitting machines and what they can do. I'm confident that you'd find a knitting machine a valuable *addition* to your hand work.

3 MACHINE KNITTING

Domestic machine knitting

Although the first domestic knitting machine appeared in Europe in the late thirties, many people have never seen a knitting machine, and have no idea what it is. The drawing in figure 29 gives a clearer idea than a photograph of what the needlebed and carriage of a single bed punchcard machine look like, but the photographs in figures 35, 46 and 57 may help you visualise the whole machine more clearly. An interesting account of the history of the domestic knitting machine is given by Kathleen Kinder in her *Resource Book for Machine Knitters* (see reading list, page 141.)

There are several different kinds of domestic knitting machine, with different capabilities, and I'll give you some idea of the various machines you can buy and what they can do. Industrial machines are as different from these as industrial weaving looms are from hand looms.

Instead of using two knitting needles to produce a

stitch, domestic knitting machines use a special needle, called a latch needle. (See figure 30.) The knitting machine is a frame of slots holding needles lined up side by side. Each of these holds one stitch. A row is worked by feeding yarn and pushing a carriage across the bed of needles. The carriage controls the movement of the needles. The four basic needle positions used in most modern machines are shown in figure 31. Where hand knitting uses different needle sizes to regulate the size of the loop produced with a particular yarn, a knitting machine has a tension dial. This can give greater variation between numbers than needle sizes can, but the fixed size of the latch needles, and their distance from each other, mean that there's a definite limit to the thickness of yarn such machines can use. Most are at their best using medium weight yarn, but they can knit what is loosely termed a 2-ply to a soft double knitting yarn. Yarn thickness is explained in more detail in Chapter 5.

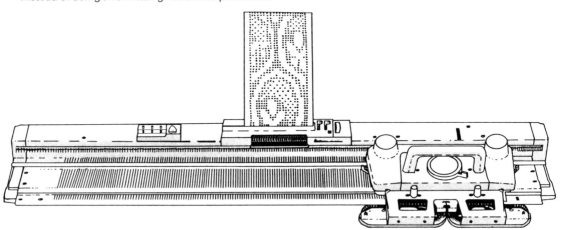

Figure 29 *A single bed automatic punchcard knitting machine. The punchcard is at the top centre, the bed of needles underneath it, with the carriage on the needlebed at the right. The pattern lever is under the handle of the carriage, the yarn feeders below the*

pattern lever and centrally placed. One row is knitted by pushing the carriage across the needlebed, the next row by pushing it across in the opposite direction. The number of needles used determines the number of stitches in the knitted piece.

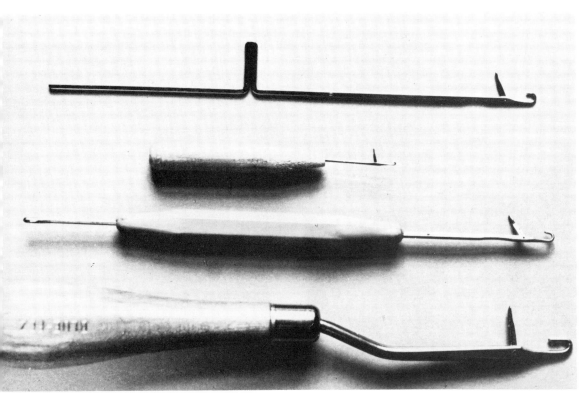

Figure 30 *Latch needles. From top to bottom: a knitting machine needle, a tool to repair ladders in stockings, a latchet tool and a carpet hook*

Left-out needles By leaving some needles *between* the working needles on the bed in the non-working position, thicker yarns can be used on a particular machine. However, the number of possible stitches is consequently fewer, and the maximum width which can be knitted correspondingly smaller. Wider gauge machines, specifically made with the thicker yarns in mind, are now available. However, they are not suited to the finer yarns. (See figure 34.)

Instruction manuals Each machine comes with a reasonably adequate manual which deals with the basic operations. These vary somewhat with the make and type of machine, so it's important to read and understand them.

Figure 31 *Basic machine needle positions on the needlebed. From top left to bottom right: the non-working position (NWP or A); the working position (WP or B); the upper working position (UPW, C or D); and the holding position (HP, D, E or F)*

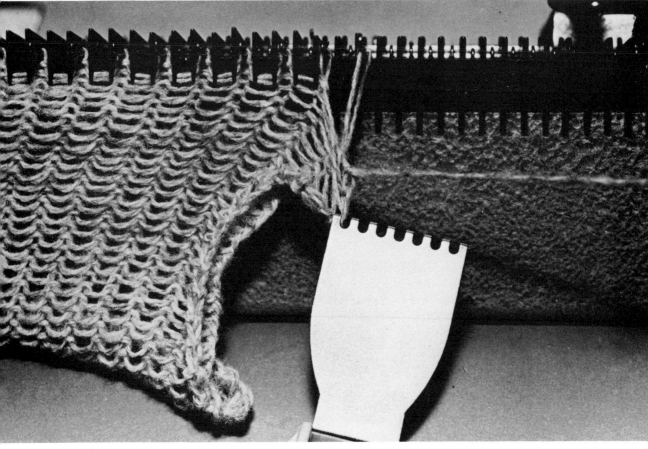

Figure 32 *Adjusting the size of cast off stitches by using a claw weight*

Hand tools A selection of hand tools is provided with each machine. These are used for shaping, casting off and working some stitch patterns manually. (See figure 60.)

Casting off by hand The basic method is given in all the manuals. In order to make a loose enough cast off, I use this method: pull the yarn down from the yarn brake and knit the first stitch of the row manually; now hang one of the small claw weights on the very edge of the garment piece; allow the weight to pull the new stitch down until there is a large enough loop for the cast off at that point. Hook this loop onto the next stitch with a transfer tool, use the yarn to form a new stitch by manually knitting through both loops, and again allow the weight to pull this new loop down sufficiently. Continuing across the row in this way, it's possible to adjust the loops so that the cast off tension is exactly what you want for that particular row in the particular yarn and pattern. (See figure 32.) Once one is practised in this method, the length of the row, which often does duty as a seam, can be adjusted precisely.

The holding position The manuals of the early knitting machines used to stress the 'unique holding position'. Modern knitting machines can do so many things that early models couldn't, and the holding position isn't automatic, but I think it's one of the most versatile methods for shaping on the machine. It depends on 'partial' knitting, that is knitting only part of a particular row and retaining the unworked stitches in the holding position, ready to be knitted again later. I have used this method in some of the garment patterns, to show how helpful it can be. It can be used, among other things, to shape shoulders, necklines, sleeveheads, toes and heels on socks and curved hems for skirts and dresses; to make horizontal darts, flared skirts, ruffles and pleats; for knitting zigzag edges; for combining colours on the diagonal. (See figure 33.)

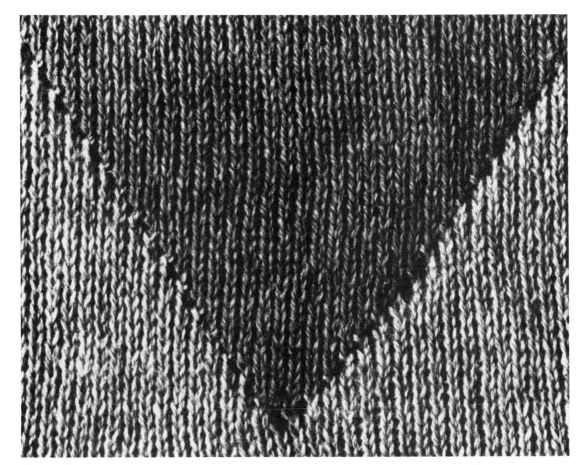

Figure 33 *Using the holding position. Diamond shapes can be knitted into the fabric without any loops appearing on the purl side*

Hems Hems are very simple to make and knit in on the machine. I prefer knitted-in hems, but it's quite simple to attach them after the garment is complete. Knitting a row of contrasting cotton thread – to be pulled out later – into the row the hem will be attached to will give a guide for keeping it straight.

Single bed machines

A single bed machine has one bed of needles. These can only produce a stocking stitch pattern, or a variation of stocking stitch. The purl side of the work faces the knitter as it comes off the machine; the machine can't automatically make knit stitches on this side of the fabric.

Basic machines The basic single bed machines consist of one needle bed, a carriage and usually a yarn tension assembly. The yarn is fed by hand or through a feeder on the carriage. These machines are relatively cheap to buy and very useful. I still have my Knitmaster 4500. It's a machine of the simplest type and the yarn is hand fed. (See figure 34.) Positioning needles by hand, you can achieve many of the patterns of the later automatic machines and, because the yarn is laid over the needles manually, you can knit with as many different colours in a row as you wish.

Don't despise a machine like this; you'd certainly find it good enough to learn machine knitting on, and, if you can get one cheaply, well worth having.

Semi-automatic machines You can buy semi-automatic machines, where you change a number of dials, press a knob or use a punchcard or needle selector to get your patterns. (See figure 35.) You may have to do this before knitting each row, which means concentrating, but again you can do a good deal with these machines. My second machine was of this type, and I found tuck lace patterns very easy to do on it; there's also a way of doing certain fairisle

Figure 34 *On the very simple, basic machines the yarn is laid across the needles by hand. Here every other needle is used in the working position*

Figure 35 *A semi-automatic machine: the Toyota 747. (Courtesy Aisin (UK) Ltd)*

patterns which isn't at all difficult, but if you're the impatient type, better opt for a fully automatic machine.

Automatic punchcard machines A modern automatic punchcard machine will do a great deal for you almost effortlessly. It has two feeders for automatic two-colour knitting and a yarn tension assembly through which the yarns are threaded and tensioned before going to the feeders. (See figures 55 and 56.) The machine uses a plastic card with blank spaces. These spaces are either left as they are or have holes punched into them, to make a pattern. The machine 'reads' the positions of the holes and blanks on the card fed into it, and 'gives' this information to the needles. The needles corresponding to the holes then perform one function, the needles corresponding to the blanks another. The way they actually knit (that is, what they do) is decided by which pattern is selected on the pattern levers, buttons or dials on the machine. The pattern

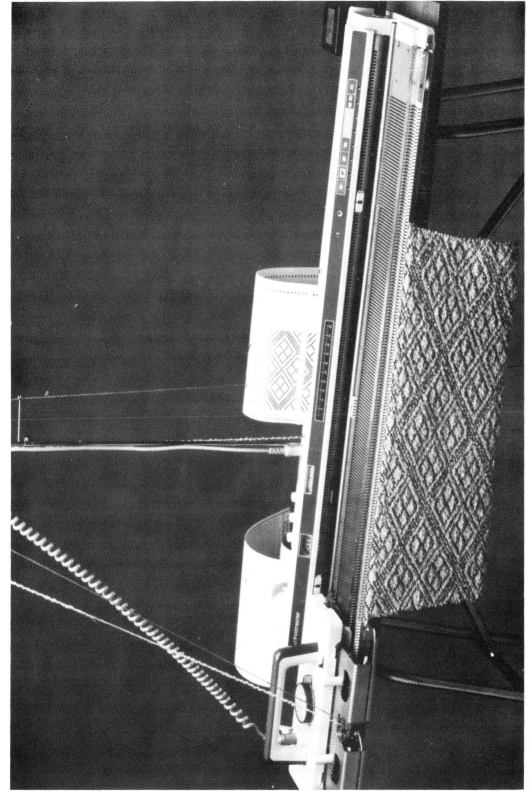

Figure 36 *The Knitmaster Electronic SK 500. (Courtesy Knitmaster Ltd)*

width, decided by the number of spaces on the card and how it is punched, is repeated across the row.

Electronic machines The latest breakthrough in knitting machines, introduced by Knitmaster in 1979, is a machine using electronic sensors to read a pattern card. Instead of punching a card, the design is drawn or traced onto a special graph paper (see figure 36) and 'read' by a 'sensor head' once the power source is switched on. The machine is able to double the width or length of a design, to make a mirror image or to change colours over in two colour knitting. Parts of the design can be placed in any part of a knitted piece and the combination of functions can produce a design 240 stitches wide and 600 rows long. However, the machine has only a 200 stitch needle bed. (See figure 37.)

I think it will be useful to give a short summary of the patterns punchcard machines can knit, and to say how easy it is to use the machines for each pattern. Some techniques for increasing the stitch pattern range are discussed in Chapter 7.

Automatic punchcard patterns

Stockinet Stockinet is the stocking stitch, or jersey, of hand knitting. (See figure 15.) It's the basic knitting machine fabric, and is worked on the punchcard machines without using a punchcard.

Fairisle Fairisle is two colour knitting on the machine. There are two feeders on the carriage for the two yarns. The pattern of the fairisle is punched into the plastic card, where the needles corresponding to the holes knit one colour, and the needles corresponding to the blanks knit the second colour. The knitting is completely automatic, and easy to do. Generally, you can only use two colours in any one row, but, if you're prepared to change the colours in either or both of the feeders when you've finished a particular row, you can use as many colours as you wish for a garment. (See plates 1, 4 and 8 facing pp 72, 73 and 97.)

Single motif This is a variation of fairisle, and is easier to do on some machines than on others. With some machines there's a simple system of knitting a chosen fairisle motif on only one part of a garment piece. On others the system can also be used to knit a particular motif pattern several times across the fabric width. You might like to have three boats across a jumper front, for instance. Motif knitting isn't difficult, but you do have to have a certain skill

Figure 37 *A garment knitted on the Knitmaster SK 500. The 'tigerskin' pattern is wide enough and long enough to cover the whole garment piece; in effect, it is motif knitting on a large scale. (Courtesy Knitmaster Ltd)*

Figure 38 *Transfer lace made on a knitting machine by using hand tools*

in machine knitting before you can do motif knitting well.

Punch lace An interesting type of fabric can be made using normal yarn in the first feeder and a transparent nylon, or very thin thread, in the second. The punchcards used for fairisle often make good punch lace patterns. It has quite a lacy look. On some machines the main yarn and the thread are knitted together on the needles corresponding to the blanks, and the thread itself is knitted on its own on the needles corresponding to the holes, according to the pattern on the punchcard. If the thread used is transparent nylon, the lace will seem much more open than if using sewing or glitter thread. (See figure 3.) For some patterns the 'wrong' side is also interesting.

Many people don't like knitting with nylon thread because it's slippery and difficult to handle. I've known knitters who've never mastered the technique adequately, others who've had no trouble so long as they used thread rather than nylon, and still others who manage quite easily. I find it's best to push the carriage across quite slowly and evenly. The edge stitches need a certain amount of care.

One other problem is that some makes of nylon thread can't be pressed at a high temperature – it simply melts away, leaving holes and dropped stitches. It's now possible to buy nylon which can cope with high temperatures, but you need to check this point when you buy.

Transfer lace Some machines can't automatically produce the sort of lace readily made in hand knitting. It's possible to use the transfer tools to make the holes by hand. However, there are machines with a special carriage called a lace carriage which does this automatically. They use special punchcards showing when to use the lace carriage. This has to be pushed across separately, so it does take longer than ordinary knitting, and you have to read the pattern on the punchcard, to tell you when, and for how many rows, to use your lace carriage. It isn't as fast or as automatic as ordinary knitting, but it does give attractive results. (See figure 38.)

pattern is formed on the purl side, where the different positions and lengths of the floats give the look of the pattern. As the yarn itself is shown off very well by this method, it's particularly effective for textured yarns, especially those where thick and thin bits alternate. (See figures 39 and 65.)

It's not all that difficult to knit slip stitch patterns, although the edge stitches need care on some machines. You will, on average, push the carriage across twice as often as in stockinet or fairisle or punch lace to get the same length of material. So it does take longer to do.

A variation is to change the colour in the feeder every few rows; the number will depend on the sort of pattern you're knitting. You'll get a fairisle effect on the knit side of the work, a needleweaving effect on the pattern or purl side.

Tuck stitch Tuck stitch can be used in many ways. It's formed by holding the yarn *on* a particular needle without knitting it, so that there's a knitted stitch as well as yarn over the chosen needles. If the pattern is punched to hold the yarn over the same needle for several rows, you get a very pronounced drawn-up effect – a tuck. Figure 40 shows a particular tuck stitch knitted in a wool yarn and in cotton. The cotton shows quite clearly how the stitch pattern is made.

On the purl side, which is the side usually considered the 'right' side, tuck stitch can give exciting textures. On the knit side, you can arrange the punchcard to produce ridges, almost like the bobble stitches of hand knitting. (See figure 4.) Many patterns produce excellent reversible fabrics. There's a lot of scope for individual design, and it's not hard to do. I've found some knitters have trouble with the yarn not staying over the needle it's supposed to tuck on; I think this is mainly because they try to knit too fast. Stitches at the edge again need extra care on some machines.

One variation of tuck stitch is tuck lace. If you

Figure 40 *Tuck stitch: this particular pattern is produced by leaving every fourth needle in the non-working position and tucking for three rows at a time on selected needles* (opposite above)

Figure 41 *Tuck lace: leaving two needles in the non-working position on either side of one working needle produces long strands. Tucked, these give a good lace effect. The central needle of three adjoining working needles can be tucked at regular intervals to produce a fabric which will fold back on itself at the side to form a quick, neat shell edging* (opposite below)

Figure 39 *Slip stitch: a pattern made on a punchcard machine*

Slip stitch Slip stitch patterns are made by letting some of the working needles stay idle. The punchcard will tell the machine on which needles to knit, and on which to hold the previous stitch without knitting. For needles which don't knit, the yarn is simply taken under the needle, as a float. The

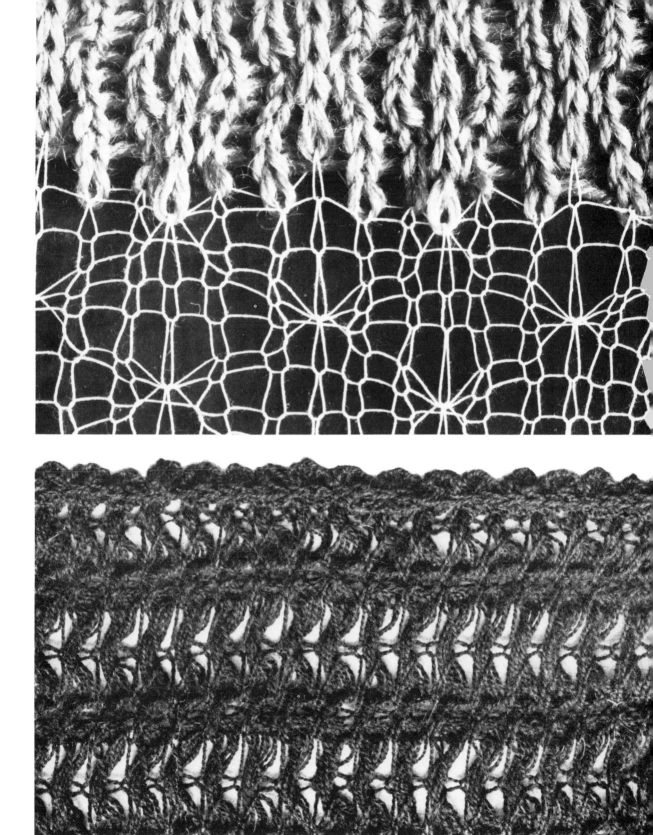

Figure 42 *The knit side of coloured tuck stitch. This sleeve top has been knitted onto the armhole edges of a sweater*

leave the needles on either side of the needles chosen for tucking in the non-working position, you will have long strands giving the impression of holes. (See figure 41.) You work out your punchcard with this in mind. It's one of my favourite ways of knitting lace. These patterns make an elastic fabric, standing out in quite pronounced relief. I've found it looks delicate but is very warm to wear.

Another variation is to change the colour in the feeder when you get to the end of a group of tuck rows. This gives a puckered fairisle on the knit side, and of course you don't get floats on the purl side; so you can use that as your pattern side. If you're thinking of using several colours for a garment anyway, it doesn't take that much longer than knitting stripes or changing colours for fairisle. What does take longer is the fact that you're shortening

the length with the tucks, so you'll have to knit more rows to the centimetre or inch than in ordinary knitting. This is true for all tuck work, not just coloured tuck patterns. (See figures 42 and 88.)

Knitweave I find this one of the most useful patterns on the machine, although it's not automatic and takes rather longer than ordinary knitting. The pattern selector is set at stockinet, and though the punchcard determines the pattern automatically, you have to insert or lower special brushes into the carriage and feed weaving yarn into the guides on the left and right of the carriage by hand. You have to change the weaving yarn from one side of the carriage to the other on each row and, as you can imagine, this slows you down. (See figure 43.)

Knitweaving isn't quite as easy as knitting; some people take a long time to get used to it. Several instruction manuals say you can use any yarn of any thickness. This isn't quite true; you can use a great many yarns and some of them can be fairly thick. But

Figure 43 *Feeding the weaving yarn by hand. The ribber attachment can be dropped sufficiently to make single bed work possible, though knitweaving is easier without the ribber attachment on the machine*

knobbly, hairy or stiff yarns may cause problems and need special techniques. I'm not saying it isn't fairly easy to learn to knitweave, but it does take a certain amount of machine knitting skill before you can use a variety of interesting weaving yarns successfully. The results are so outstanding, in my view, that I've included a special section on how to use this method of machine knitting in Chapter 7.

Plating Some Knitmaster punchcard models have a third space, behind the first feeder on the carriage. This can be used for fine yarns to 'plate' with the main yarn, to create an interesting reversible fabric with one or other yarn predominating on each side. It can be used for stockinet or tuck settings on the carriage.

Punchcards

The machines come with a pre-punched set of cards. There are 20 cards or more, and they give a good selection of patterns to start with.

The width of the card is restricted – to 24 spaces on most machines. Pattern repeats of 24, 12, 8, 6, 4, 3 and 2 can be used with these, and a very large variety of patterns is possible. Though the width of the pattern is restricted, you can add as many cards as you wish to increase the length. Whatever length you choose, provided the cards are long enough, you can fasten their ends into a cylinder shape, so that they revolve and repeat the pattern automatically. (See figure 44.)

It's also possible to set the mechanism so that a single row is repeated as often as you wish. Some machines have a lever which can be set to repeat each pattern row twice, automatically elongating the pattern.

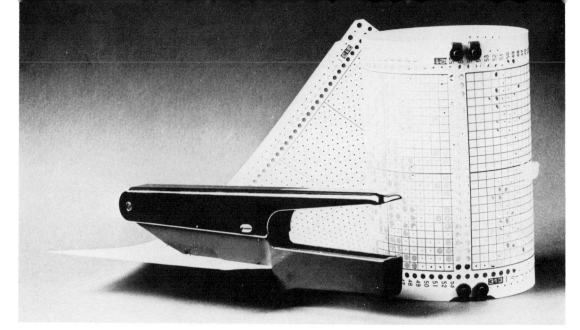

Figure 44 *The hand puncher is shown with a blank punchcard. The punched card on the right has been joined into a cylinder shape by the clips shown at top and bottom* (above)

Figure 45 *The Passap Duomatic 80. The 40–space punchcard is shown at the bottom left, and the automatic four-colour changer on the right. (Courtesy Bogod Machine Co Ltd) (below)*

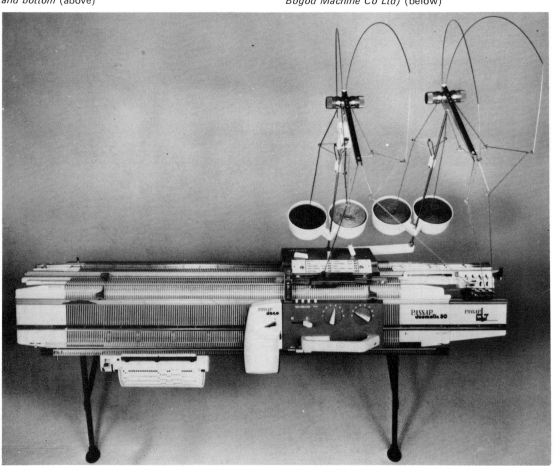

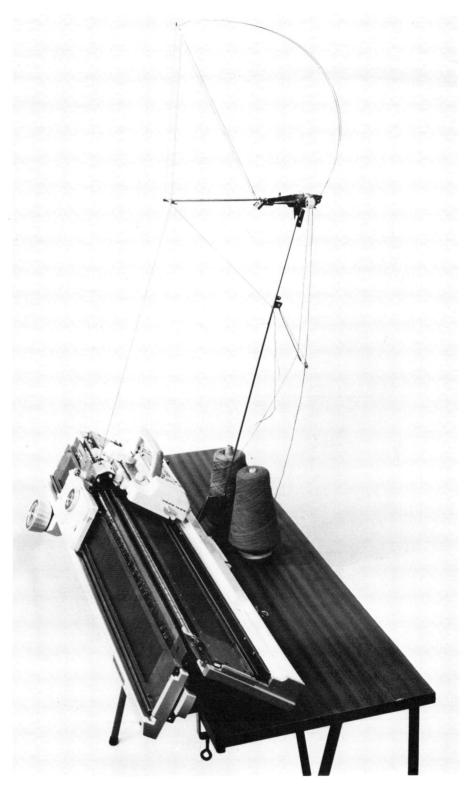

Figure 46 *The Singer Memomatic KE 2400 with ribber attachment (Courtesy The Singer Co (UK) Ltd)*

Figure 47 *The half-pitch position: the ribber needles are shown between the main bed needles*

Once you've got used to how the punchcards work you can buy a punch and blank cards, and either punch your own designs or buy printed designs which you can punch out on the cards. (See figure 118.) 'Pattern Library' books are available from knitting machine suppliers.

Punching you own designs for fairisle and working out how to make new patterns for the other stitches is one of the creative outlets in automatic machine knitting. Graph paper is useful for working out preliminary sketches for your designs, but the shapes can be misleading as they will usually be too elongated. This is because there are more rows than stitches to the unit length for most knitting tensions.

Double bed machines

The machines discussed so far can only automatically do stocking stitch and patterns based on stocking stitch. There is a way of doing knit and purl stitches in the same row automatically. In order to have knit as well as purl stitches facing the knitter, a second needle bed has to be provided. This second bed has needles pointing in the opposite direction to the ones in the first bed, and can therefore produce knit instead of purl stitches in the fabric facing the knitter. There's a carriage for each bed, but they're connected and pushed across in one movement. The fabric is produced between the two beds, and, on most machines, has to have weights attached to pull it clear of the needlebeds. (See figure 45.) This two bed arrangement is called a double bed machine, and you can buy these complete or turn a single bed machine into a double bed one by buying a second needle bed, often called a ribber. The single bed machine must be of the type which can have a ribber added. (See figure 46.)

A quite new category of machine knitting is opened up with double bed machines. The function of the second bed is not merely to produce ribbed fabrics; it can do far more than that.

Half-pitch lever The space, or pitch, between the needles on a single bed machine is wide enough to allow the second bed to be arranged so that its needles aren't opposite but between the needles of the first bed. (See figure 47.) This is made possible by the half-pitch lever and, if the needles are set at the half-pitch position, the number of needles which can be used for knitting is effectively doubled. Fine yarns must be used.

Tubular and half-tubular fabric The carriage controls can be set so that the ribber and main bed each knit on alternate rows. This facility can be used in two ways: in the first, tubular or circular stocking stitch fabric can be produced completely automatically. In the second, by adjusting the controls on the carriage after every two rows, knitting which is open at one end can be produced. In effect, the width of stocking stitch fabric can be doubled. Some double bed machines are able to make stitch patterns at the same time as producing tubular and half-tubular fabric. (See figure 48.)

Swing or racking handle Apart from the half-pitch lever, some machines also have a racking handle. This can shift or 'swing' the ribber bed one whole pitch at a time either to the left or right, in either pitch position. In this way it's possible to knit a diagonal pattern into the fabric. There's a limit to the number of shifts, but five pitches in either direction are quite common. (See figure 49.)

Patterns on different pitch positions Patterns can be worked over both needle beds, with the ribber set in the half-pitch position, or adjusted to be used with the needles in the main and ribber beds directly opposite each other. In this second position the needles in the working position on the main bed *must* be opposite needles in the non-working position on the ribber bed, and vice versa; otherwise the needles will clash. The first arrangement is for fabrics worked on both beds and for tubular and wide fabrics. The full needle setting in the half-pitch position produces a full needle rib fabric, very similar to single rib. The second arrangement is often used for thicker yarns and for fabrics knitted on the main bed only, after a part has been knitted on the two beds. The ribber needles can then be transferred manually to the main machine, and the non-working needles corresponding to the ribber needles brought forward to receive the ribber stitches. In this way the same number of stitches will be used for the single as well as the double bed work, which is normally desirable. The ribber can be lowered and single bed work carried out after the stitches have been transferred. (See figure 43.)

Figure 48 *A piece of tubular fabric made on a single bed machine with a ribber attachment*

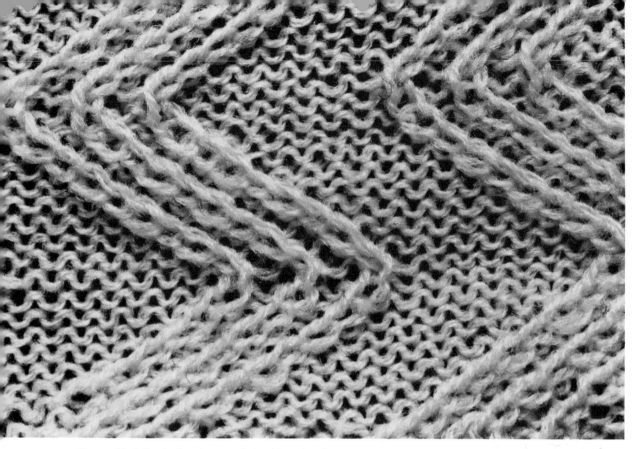

Figure 49 *A 'herringbone' pattern knitted by using the swing handle on a single bed machine with a ribber attachment*

Stitch patterns

Rib stitches Single, double, and two knit, one purl ribs are easy to set up for most double bed knitting. All other simple rib stitches are possible, but the needle selection may have to be set manually after the cast-on rows have been knitted.

Swinger or diagonal stitches All kinds of fascinating herringbone fabrics can be made by using the swinger or racking handle. This has to be done manually on a rota basis, but the results are so interesting that many people gladly take the extra trouble. Added concentration is necessary, especially as the edge stitches may have to be adjusted manually between the beds. (See figure 49.)

Punch tuck patterns If the main bed is an automatic punchcard machine, many of the tuck patterns can be used for that bed, while the ribber bed knits as usual. Care has to be taken to programme the cards correctly.

Ribber tucking Some ribbers can be set to tuck on every stitch in the working position on the ribber. Automatic pattern ribs can be made in this way. (See figure 50.)

Drive lace knitting Ribbers can be used to make a type of lace fabric, similar to the drop or spider stitch of hand knitting. Some of the modern ribbers have facilities for making this type of fabric semi-automatically.

Pile knitting Some ribbers also have facilities for making a type of pile fabric. Here a pattern of raised loops stands out from the reverse stocking stitch base. A second yarn is used to make the loops, so the fabrics can be made in one or two colours. Quite fascinating patterns can be made and, if you're particularly interested in pile fabric, you need to ask whether the particular ribber available for the machine you're thinking of buying can make it.

Starting with a single bed machine and adding a ribber later is a very good idea for people who wish to find out if they'll enjoy machine knitting. Double bed knitting needs a reasonable skill in machine knitting, not because it's particularly difficult but because you need to be familiar with knitting

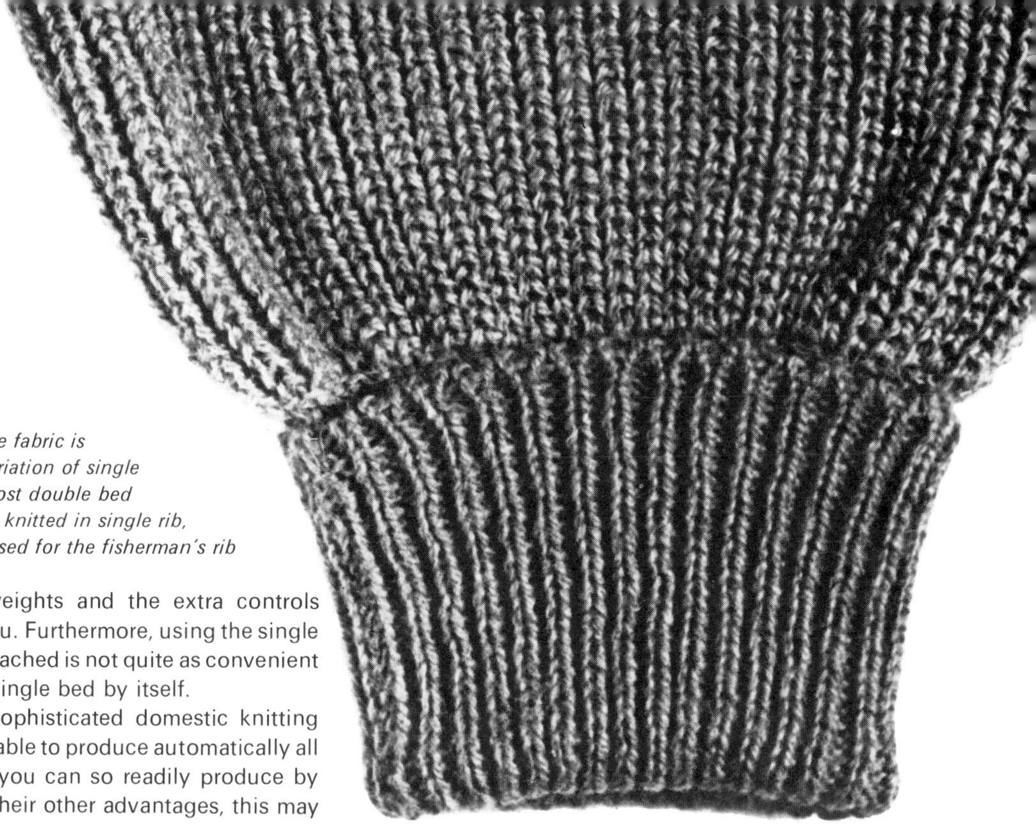

Figure 50 *The sleeve fabric is*
'fisherman's rib', a variation of single
rib easily made on most double bed
machines. The cuff is knitted in single rib,
on half the stitches used for the fisherman's rib

machines if the weights and the extra controls aren't to confuse you. Furthermore, using the single bed with a ribber attached is not quite as convenient as knitting on the single bed by itself.

Even the most sophisticated domestic knitting machines won't be able to produce automatically all the stitch patterns you can so readily produce by hand but, with all their other advantages, this may hardly concern you.

Advantages of machine knitting

When the machine has been set up, pushing the carriage across once will knit one whole *row* across the complete needlebed in ordinary machine work, and pushing it or another carriage across again will knit one row in more complicated patterns. Clearly, particularly for long rows, this is very much faster than a series of actions for a single *stitch*. Speed, then, is a considerable advantage in machine knitting; work which would take several days or even weeks done by hand can be done in a very few hours on a machine.

The punchcard and electronic machines make certain patterns as quick to knit as stocking stitch, and ribbers extend the pattern range still further. However, it isn't just a mechanical matter. You'll find that, though some knitting machines are better than others, what really counts is the person who uses them – just as in any other craft. A machine won't take away your creativity; on the contrary, it may increase it.

Technology has given us many machines which make life easier. The typewriter I use is a great boon; I don't say that I don't need to know how to write by hand, or that I don't quite often do it, but for legibility and speed it simply doesn't compare with typing. I had to buy the typewriter, and I had to learn

to use it; but once I'd done that, I had, effectively, increased my speed of writing and, as a result, the amount I actually wrote.

These are some of the reasons why I think you too will come to want a knitting machine. Just as the typewriter doesn't write by itself, the knitting machine won't craft by itself. You must feed in the ideas, the patterns, and the combinations of yarns in an adequate way. The machine will merely carry out your work quickly, meticulously and evenly.

We don't all have the same manual skills. In the past you needed to 'sew a fine seam' to be good at needlework. Now you can learn how to use a sewing machine; you still need skill, but it's a different sort of skill and, I think, more universal. With the coming of the domestic knitting machine, you don't have to be good at one row knit, one row purl. Any knitting machine will do that for you. There will be some limits to the yarns it can use and the width it can knit, but these don't matter much. The important thing is that it will do the main body of knitting for you more quickly and probably more evenly than you could do it yourself.

This frees you for much more creative work. It gives you the chance to earn money if you wish. It certainly brings knitting for a whole family well within your scope.

Using machines

Don't say you're no good at using machines; I doubt if that's true, anyway. Think of the ones you already use: cameras, perhaps; washing machines, motor mowers, vacuum cleaners, cars. . . . We live in a machine age. You don't have to be a mechanical genius; anyone can learn to use machines and knitting machines aren't all that difficult to use. If you actually like machines, as I do, you can make them 'sing'. People who have never considered the craft of knitting before get involved with these machines and are prepared to learn the necessary handwork in order to use their machines to the full. If you don't particularly like machines, think of it the other way round: you will learn to use the machine because it extends your handwork.

Of course you can knit creatively by hand, but it's a long time before your vision of the article becomes the article itself. The machine increases your speed and so allows you to invent more. You can quickly create new fabrics – exclusive to you. You can combine yarns and colours, thread them up in novel ways, join completely different textures in new combinations. There are so many ways of doing this, you're bound to make something unique. Not just clothing: chair covers, cushion covers, curtains, rugs, table cloths and napkins, wall hangings – anything you can do in fabric. You can never tell what's going to work and what isn't. This is where the thrill of discovery comes in. The fact that you have two colours in front of you doesn't tell you what they'll be like knitted together – as Jacquard, as knitweave, as punch lace, as single motif. It depends on pattern, texture, size . . . and what you put it with! So it's hard work, and it's time consuming, but, once you've found a fabric you like, you can plan how to use it.

A small pattern piece won't always tell you what a finished garment in the fabric will look like. After you've made the first large piece you may not like the result. Fortunately knitting on a machine is so fast it's not too much trouble to start again.

When you've finished with the main part of the knitting on the machine, you can add further creative touches by inventing trimmings in crochet, in knitting, in macramé, with embroidery, or even on the machine itself.

You can use your trials and errors for collage work, for making patchwork cushions or bedspreads, for covering buttons or making soft toys and dolls' clothes. You need not waste anything, and you don't need patterns. One idea will lead to another.

4 TOOLING UP

The tools
Knitting needles

Pencils, pens, hat pins – many long, thin objects can be used as a knitting needle or pin of a sort. For good, even knitting, you have to use something a little better. A good knitting needle has a number of important attributes: it should be light enough in weight not to tire you while you're working; smooth enough not to catch on the slightest piece of fibre; round-ended enough for comfortable knitting; strong enough not to break under the weight of heavy fabric; the right colour to show up well against dark stitches, which are the hardest to see; coated to a high enough standard, so that the needle doesn't taint even the lightest yarns; of the right length to be comfortable for the knitter; and, finally, of the right gauge to produce the correct tension for the knitter and the yarn being used.

This may sound a tall order, but the leading brands of knitting needles are all quite excellent, and an investment in a comprehensive set of knitting needles of different sizes will give you scope for experimenting with different yarns and tensions, and the opportunity to find the right tools for your purposes. It helps to keep your needles in a sturdy case to prevent them getting scratched. Figure 51 shows the different types of needles.

Knob-ended knitting needles, sold in pairs, can generally be found in 35 cm (14 in.), 30 cm (12 in.) and 25 cm (10 in.) lengths, in metric sizes 2 mm to 10 mm (US sizes 00 to 15).

Maxi needles are larger than ordinary knob-ended needles – in the range of 15 mm to 25 mm ($\frac{1}{2}$ in. to 1 in.) in diameter.

Figure 51 *From top left to bottom right: knob ended needles, maxi needles, a set of four double-pointed needles, needle gauge, twin pins, short double-pointed needles, two sizes of crochet hook and a stitch holder*

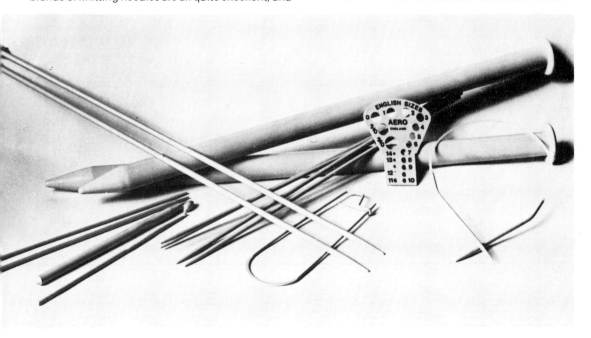

Double-pointed needles, that is needles with points at both ends, are usually sold in sets of four, in lengths of 30 cm (12 in.) 23 cm (9 in.) and 18 cm (7 in.). The generally available sizes range from metric 2 mm to 5 mm (US sizes 00 to 7).

Cable needles are short, double-pointed needles often sold in sets of three, to use when knitting with needles ranging from metric sizes 2 mm to 7·5 mm (US sizes 00 to 12).

Circular or twin pins can be bought in lengths from 40 cm (16 in.) to 102 cm (42 in.), but the most readily available lengths are 40 cm (16 in.), 61 cm (24 in.) and 76 cm (30 in.). A large range of lengths is necessary; short lengths for a relatively small number of stitches, long ones for large numbers of stitches. The number of stitches each needle can hold depends on the yarn and tension. You would need about 80 stitches to be able to use a 40 cm (16 in.) length for a tension of 5 stitches to 2·5 cm (1 in.).

Sets of knob-ended needles, in 35 cm (14 in.) and 30 cm (12 in.) lengths, are readily available in plastic cases. Sizes are usually from metric 2·75 mm to 7 mm (US sizes 1 to 11). Circular and double-pointed needles can, of course, be used for flat knitting. Some shops sell rubber ends to fit onto one end of a pointed needle, so that it can conveniently be used for flat knitting. You can use small corks in an emergency.

Stitch holders look like large safety pins. (See figure 51.) *Stitch keepers* can be bought or made by putting a knob (or cork) on both ends of a double-pointed needle. I find circular needles good substitutes; the work is always ready to knit off in either direction and the needles automatically curve round so that stitches don't easily drop off.

Needle gauge

A particularly useful gadget is called a needle gauge. This will not only give you the size of knitting needles which have lost their markings or, being pointed at both ends, don't have them; it will automatically convert the UK system, now being replaced, to the metric system. The gauge will measure needles with diameters between 2 mm and 10 mm on one side, and give the non-metric UK equivalent sizes on the other. (See figure 51.) The table following gives roughly equivalent metric, UK and US sizes.

UK	14	13	12	11	10	9
USA	00	0	1	2	3	4
mm	2	2·25	2·75	3	3·25	3·75

UK	8	7	6	5	4	3	2	1
USA	5	6	7	8	9	10	11	12
mm	4	4·5	5	5·5	6	6·5	7	7·5

Crochet hooks

Apart from substituting a comfortable hook for a comfortable point, crochet hooks have the same requirements for excellence, and are made by the manufacturers who produce knitting needles. Again, a full range of sizes readily available in a neat case makes it easier to find your own style of crafting. Little-used sizes always come in useful at some time, and, as I mentioned in Chapter 1, the original investment is not high. Metric sizes are now generally used, ranging from 2 mm to 7·5 mm in diameter (US sizes B/1 to K10$\frac{1}{4}$). The gauge used for knitting needles can be used for crochet hooks.

Sewing needles

For sewing knitted fabrics, whether by hand or machine, the new *ball-point* needles are a great advance on the sharp-pointed ones; they don't snag the yarn or the fabric. *Tapestry needles* with a wide eye and a blunt point – available in a good range of sizes – are excellent for hand sewing with knitting yarn. (See figure 52.)

Glass-headed pins show up better than dressmaker's pins in a domestically produced knitted fabric; the material is thicker than most woven materials, and the loops tend to hide ordinary pins.

Small accessories

You'll need something to measure your tension swatch. I find a *ruler*, marked in both centimetres and inches, better than a tape measure, because it doesn't stretch or bend; and a transparent one is easier to use. You'll also need a good *tape measure*, for body measurements. Choose one which doesn't stretch easily and, again, marked in both centimetres and inches. This makes it easy to convert from one measuring system to the other. A sharp pair of *cutting-out scissors* is essential if you're intending to use knitted fabric for dressmaking; the sharper the

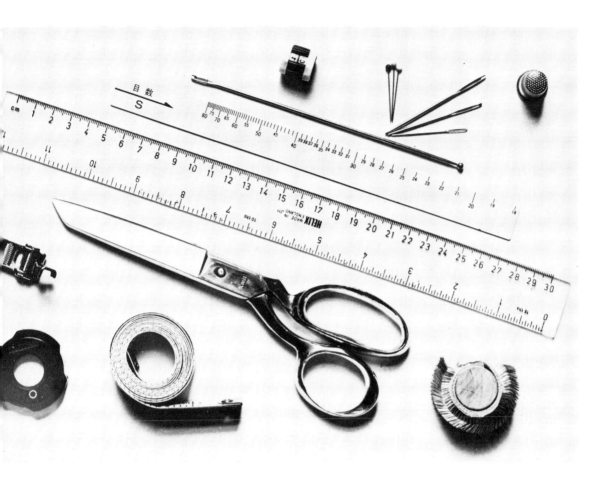

Figure 52 *From top left to bottom right: a stitch counter, glass headed pins, tapestry needles, thimble, round-ended bodkin, the 'green ruler', transparent ruler, cutting out scissors, roller foot, sewing machine cam for making a stretch stitch, tape measure, teazel brush*

scissors, the less likelihood of the stitches being pulled when cut, with the danger of stitches running.

A *latchet tool*, (see figure 30) though a machine knitting tool, is also the best one for the hand knitter to use for picking up dropped stitches. A *bodkin* with a rounded knob at the end is invaluable for threading elastic, ribbon or cording through knitted or crocheted fabric without snagging it. A *row register* keeps a tally of the number of rows you've knitted. *Teazel brushes*, the substitutes for the wild thistle heads which were used to raise the pile on fabrics, are inexpensive tools for fluffing up fabrics made of yarns such as angora, mohair and some of the Shetland wools. Figure 52 shows these accessories.

Sewing machines

Sewing machines can be a great help in making up the knitted fabric pieces into completed garments. The seams are quicker to make, they don't depend on neat hand stitching and are, generally, tear proof. However, sewing machines don't all perform the same functions. Some are *straight-stitch* machines which sew straight seams both backwards and forwards. The longest stitch can be used to seam up domestically produced knitted fabric, but these seams are liable to come undone because the stitches break when the very flexible fabric is stretched. It's possible to buy an attachment which will make a zigzag stitch by shifting the fabric from side to side while the machine is sewing.

Plain *zigzag* machines have a 'swing' needle which can go from side to side as well as backwards and forwards. The zigzag stitch, though not making a continuous seam, is a flexible stitch, and a narrow zigzag used on a knitted fabric will be more successful than a straight stitch. A wide zigzag can also

Figure 53 *A sewing machine stretch stitch, and back stitch made by hand*

oversew rough edges, which is useful for cut and sew methods of preparing knitwear.

Semi-automatic and *automatic* machines can produce a more complex type of stitch; the swing needle can go backwards as well as forwards automatically, so that it can produce machine embroidery and 'stretch' stitches, that is stitches which 'give' with flexible fabrics. I use an Elna SU machine which has several cams for stretch stitches; these make a straight seam and overlock at the same time. I find it excellent for making up knitwear quickly. (See figure 53.)

A *roller foot* is a simple attachment for a sewing machine. (See figure 52.) The knitted fabric can be eased under the foot by slightly lifting the two edges to be sewn as you feed them in. The attachment stops the fabric from being stretched out of shape as it's sewn.

Domestic versions of *link* and *interlocking* machines can now be bought; these are the types of machine used by knitwear manufacturers to make seams in knitwear.

Pressing machines

Provided a damp cloth is used for pressing, any iron with adjustable temperature will do for pressing knitwear. However, I don't, in general, recommend pressing, as so many yarns contain some synthetics better left unpressed. Apart from that, knitted stitch patterns are easily flattened out of shape. Chapter 8 will explain the method I use instead.

Some flatbed pressing machines are available which will press fabric produced by the metre or yard on a knitting machine. These are great time savers for suitable fabrics.

Knitting machines

The following is a short list of some of the knitting machines available in the UK, and of some in the US and in Australia at the present time. The details given are taken from the latest information sent by the manufacturers. For accurate information on the current models and prices it's best to contact the manufacturers or their importers direct. Prices change so quickly that it simply isn't practical to quote them in a book. However, to give you some idea of the costs involved: as of 1980, an automatic punchcard machine costs roughly the same as a large fridge-freezer, a medium sized colour TV set, or an expensive automatic camera. This is for the basic single bed machine without accessories.

Domestic knitting machines are made in Japan, Switzerland and France, and are available from six manufacturers in the UK. The manufacturers sometimes sell their machines through importers and distributors, and complications can be introduced because the machines are sold under different trade names in different countries. Furthermore, not all the models are available everywhere. The relevant present UK addresses, as well as some US addresses, are given at the end of this book.

Because of these difficulties it's essential to find a good dealer if you're new to machine knitting; in

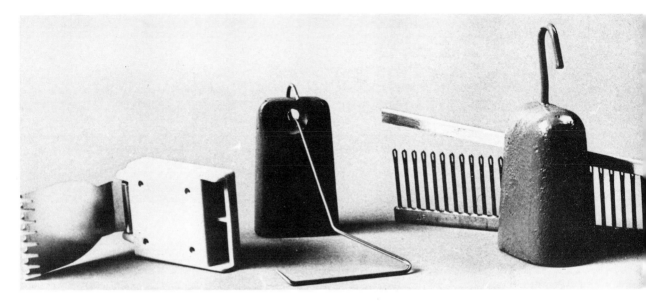

Figure 54 *From left to right: small claw weight, edge weight for ribber, weight used with most ribbers, garter bar with holder to secure stitches*

most cases he'll see that you get some sort of instruction, whatever the policy of the manufacturer or the company marketing the machine.

At the moment there's no *one* machine which can produce all the patterns which the domestic knitting machines available at present are capable of. A short summary of what each of the four current punchcard models can do, and a brief guide to two double bed machines, follows below. By the time you read this, new models will doubtless have appeared, so you should check what new features these have. In fact, the new *one action* automatic lacemaker from Knitmaster is due in September 1980. All the single bed punchcard machines use interchangeable 24-space punchcards, but patterning starts from different lines on the card: line 4 for Singer, 5 for Knitmaster and 7 for Brother and Toyota. Three of the four punchcard models select the patterning needles to the C position. (See figure 31.) This means that patterns can be adjusted very easily by hand, by pushing some of these needles back to the B position. A number of interesting semi-automatic patterns can be worked in this way.

Knitmaster machines select the needles and set them back to the B position automatically, so it isn't possible to adjust these needles manually. Consequently semi-automatic patterning is restricted to needles pushed to the D or holding position.

Knitmaster machines are the only ones which do punch lace and plate knitting, but there's no transfer lace carriage.

All the single bed machines can have ribber attachments added to turn them into double bed machines. All of them use weights for double bed knitting (see figure 54); some use cast-on combs for single bed work. Small weights are often advisable for pattern knitting on the single bed. All these machines have beds of 200 needles each, and a fabric width of up to 91 cm (36 in.) can be made on these. The width depends on the yarn used, and the tension and pattern selected as well as on the number of needles.

Brother KH 830 (Brother US, Brother Australia) This machine can knit stockinet, fairisle, tuck, slip, knitweave and two types of transfer lace. Its lace carriage can be set to do fine lace as well as transfer lace by slipping one stitch over two adjacent needles. There is a colour changer attachment for the single as well as the double bed. The single motif is worked manually by adjusting the needles in C position. The ribber doesn't do pile knitting. A cast-on comb is used. The 'Knitleader' pattern charting device uses full scale patterns. (See figure 55.)

Knitmaster 326 (Studio US, Silver Australia) knits fairisle, stockinet, slip, tuck, punch lace, plate knitting and knitweave. Transfer lace cannot be produced automatically, but the pattern can be worked manually. It's not necessary to use cast-on combs. The ribber attachment is very versatile and will do pile knitting and drive lace. Four-colour changers

Figure 55 *The Brother KH 830, with punchcard on the right and a ribbing attachment fitted to the machine. (Courtesy Jones Sewing Machine Co Ltd)*

Figure 56 *The Knitmaster 326, with the 'Knitradar' half-size pattern charting device shown on the left, the punchcard in the centre, and the carriage on the right. (Courtesy Knitmaster Ltd)*

are available but need the ribber attachment for both single and double bed work. Single motif or selected motifs are very easy to make by using the 'magic cams'. Tucking can be done over two adjacent stitches. The 'Knitradar' charting device comes with the machine; it uses half-scale patterns. (See figure 56.)

Singer Memomatic KE 2400 (not available in the US) will knit stockinet, fairisle, slip, tuck, knitweave and transfer lace with the lace carriage

provided. The punchcard mechanism is mounted on the carriage instead of the needlebed. No cast-on comb is necessary. The ribbing attachment comes complete with a four-colour changer, but cannot be set to do pile knitting. (See figure 46.)

Toyota KS 787 (Toyota US) This machine is the only single bed automatic punchcard machine currently available which has manual push button pattern selection as well as punchcard patterning. A cast-on comb is used. The single motif can be

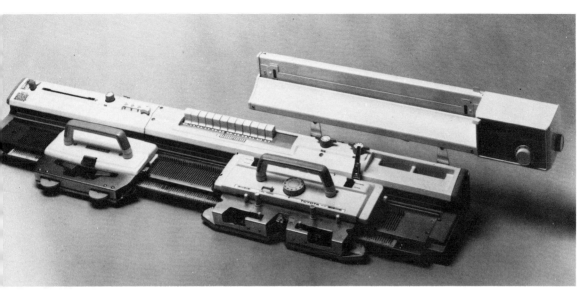

Figure 57 *The Toyota KS 787, with lace carriage on the left, push buttons in the centre, 'Knit Tracer' full size pattern charting device at the right back and carriage on the right. (Courtesy Aisin (UK) Ltd)*

produced in one position by the turn of a dial, but spaced, selected motifs have to be done manually. The machine can knit stockinet, tuck, slip, fairisle, knitweave and transfer lace with the lace carriage supplied. A ribber is available, but it cannot do pile knitting. The 'Simulknit' attachment makes it possible to knit floatless double fairisle knits using a fairisle punchcard; this is a different system from the 'stripers' available for other machines. The 'Knit Tracer' pattern charting device, supplied with the machine, uses full scale patterns on the tracer sheet. (See figure 57.)

Passap Duomatic 80 This is a double bed machine using 179 needles on each bed. It doesn't need to use a cast-on comb or weights. Jersey can be knitted on one bed, or as a tube on both beds, or by leaving one seam of the tube open to make a wider fabric. Some stitch patterns can be worked on the tubular and semi-tubular fabric.

Patterning is done by a pattern selector dial on the machine. This can produce a variety of simple fairisle, tuck, slip and fancy rib patterns, as well as Jacquard, that is fairisle with woven-in floats. Aran effects in the row are possible by setting the needles and 'pushers' up in various ways along the row.

To increase the pattern range, and to make it completely automatic, it is possible to buy a 40-space punchcard attachment; this can be used to make more intricate Jacquard and other designs, with a very wide pattern repeat. Single motif is also possible and a four-colour changer is available. This can be used to knit two, three or four colours into one row. A transfer lock attachment can be bought to make transfer stitch patterns, either as lace or for designs such as moss stitch. (See figure 45.)

Superba S-42 This machine is a double bed machine using 180 needles on each bed. The patterning system is completely different from that of the other knitting machines mentioned: the patterning is done by setting pegs in a selection box rather than punching out a punchcard. This gives considerable scope for creative patterning, but it takes a little longer to do and to get used to. The designs can be up to 38 stitches in width provided they're symmetrical. The machine knits stockinet, slip, tuck, knitweave and fairisle as well as different rib stitches, and tubular and semi-tubular knitting. It can do single motif and weave in the floats of fairisle knitting, producing a Jacquard fabric. A high speed unit is available for semi-industrial knitting speeds to make jersey and ribbed fabrics, and a garter bar accessory makes it possible to do garter stitch, moss stitch and other transfer stitch patterns, and transfer lace. A cast-on comb is used to start the work and weights are used during the knitting.

Knitting machine accessories

Ribber In order to turn a single bed machine into a double one, a ribber attachment can be bought, as already discussed in Chapter 3.

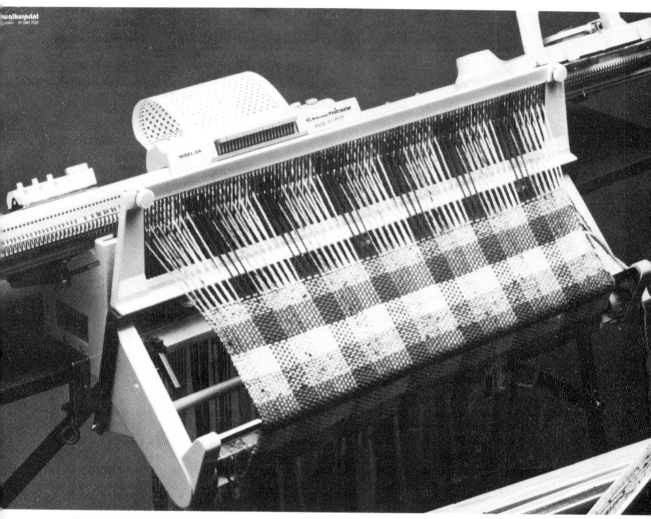

Figure 58 *A weaving attachment: this can be fitted to most single bed punchcard machines. (Courtesy Knitmaster Ltd)*

Colour Changer I've said that changing colours in the feeder to make stripes, or coloured tuck stitch, or fairisle with more than two colours, is rather tedious. A colour changing attachment is available for some single bed and most double bed machines, which lets you choose up to four colours automatically.

It's possible to weave in the floats of fairisle knitting on a double bed machine. The fabric produced is called *Jacquard* and is made by using the full needle rib setting on a double bed machine. The punchcard is punched out so that each pattern row is punched twice – once in the ordinary way and once with the holes and blanks reversed. (See Mary Weaver – *The Ribbing Attachment Part I*, Weaver-

knits Ltd, 1974 for full details). One yarn colour only is used at any one time, but the colours are changed every two rows. The fabric produced in this way will have the fairisle pattern on one side and stockinet in a two-row stripe sequence on the other, with no loose floats. An automatic colour changer – often called a 'striper' – speeds up this type of work considerably. Only fine yarns should be used.

Charting device Instead of using a printed garment pattern, some machines have systems for reading a pattern while you're knitting. Special paper or plastic sheets with boldly marked shapes are fed into the systems and these show you where to increase and decrease as you knit. The scale of the pattern varies with the make of the system. Provided you draw the correct shapes, you can use these systems to knit a favourite pattern in a large range of sizes without having to work out the adjustments arithmetically. You can even use the system to knit from unusual angles – sideways, say, or from a corner. And you can feed any special shapes you like into the machine, by drawing them to scale. Full-scale models give you the chance to use ordinary dressmaking patterns merely by tracing them onto the special paper or plastic. (See figures 56 and 57.)

Weaving attachment A weaving device can be attached to most single bed knitting machines; this allows you to use their patterning systems for weaving. (See figure 58.)

Electric motors It's possible to fit an electric motor to some of the knitting machines. This means the carriage is taken backwards and forwards for you. In other words, you can have either a manual or

an electric knitting machine in the same way that you can have a manual or electric sewing machine.

Lubricators Wax discs and lubricating sprays are available to prepare rough or fancy yarns for smooth action on the needles. The yarn is sprayed with a special lubricant or threaded through a wax disc. Ordinary candles or night lights with their wicks taken out can be used for waxing, but these won't fit onto the yarn assemblies or woolwinders for automatic waxing.

Winders It's essential to have a gadget called a *woolwinder*. (See figure 59.) This rewinds balled yarn or knitting you want to unravel into a suitable form for machine knitting. Balled yarn has to be rewound because it won't unwind fast enough for the speed of knitting on a machine. The rewinding must be done slowly enough not to create too much

Figure 59 *Woolwinder and yarns wound for machine knitting. From left to right: a 'pull ball', sewing thread reel, medium cone, yarn ball wound on woolwinder, thread on a small cone, yarn on a large cone*

tension in the centre of the new ball; otherwise it, too, won't unwind fast enough for machine knitting. *Conewinders* can also be bought.

Wool in skeins isn't all that common any more, but occasionally one comes across it. Using a *skeinwinder* makes it easy to wind directly from the skein to the woolwinder. It will also re-skein unravelled yarn so that it can be washed or steamed before re-winding and re-knitting. If you like to dye your own yarn, as suggested in Chapter 5, you'll find a skeinwinder invaluable, as balled or coned yarns need to be skeined before they're dyed.

Garter bar A garter bar is used for taking all the stitches in use off the machine, turning the knitting, and putting them all back on again. It can also be used as a stitch holder for separate garment sections to be knitted in later. There are several lengths, so you needn't struggle with a long bar for turning, say, 30 stitches only. (See figure 54.)

Knitting table A specially made table to which you can clamp the machine is a great help. It's narrow, so that you can put cones on the floor behind the machine for faster and vertical unwinding, which makes for much faster knitting. As it takes up little room, it can more readily be set up in a permanent position.

Extra tension assembly An extra tension assembly to give a choice of two more colours for knitting can be fitted to many machines. Even without a colour changer it's a great help to be able to change up to four yarns in the feeder without having to unthread one and replace it with another in the tension assembly. That is quite a performance, and guiding the yarn through the feeder by hand is only suitable for a very few rows or for knitweaving.

Handy punch You can buy a gadget to punch out your own punchcards. Blank cards are available at knitting centres. Punching cards isn't my favourite pastime, but it's essential for working out one's own designs for punchcard knitting. When my children were small they loved punching the holes, so that's how I used to get my cards done! Try someone else's child if you haven't got one handy. (See figure 44.)

Weights Many machines are equipped with two small weights as standard accessories. However, a number of stitch patterns need extra weights, and I suggest you equip yourself with not less than six small claw weights. They're useful for holding down the material when using the holding position and, among other things, for knitting tuck stitch patterns. (See figure 54.)

Choosing a knitting machine
Second-hand machines

You can often get a cheap, second-hand machine because someone hasn't coped with theirs, and if you're short of cash that's one way to start. However, there are one or two things to bear in mind if you intend to buy second-hand.

Many people don't use knitting machines properly. They use force, and this may have damaged the machine quite badly, though you can't actually see the damage. Find out why the machine is being sold; get the owner to talk about his or her knitting experiences. You'll soon know all you need to know.

There are also the less successful models. The seller may be perfectly good at machine knitting, but the machine's a dud. There are some; it's not that they don't work, but they take more effort than they should. Get the seller to show you how to work the machine, and, if it seems rather trickier than the ones you've seen demonstrated in stores, think twice before you buy. You might be able to arrange a trial; unlikely, but it's worth suggesting.

Finally, it might be a model for which spare parts are hard to come by. You'll need to get needles to replace damaged ones and a few other bits and pieces.

On the other hand you might come across a bargain. Some people don't even unpack their machine; I know it sounds implausible, but it's true. Whatever second-hand machine you do buy, make certain you have the instruction manual to go with it. Even an experienced machine knitter can't know exactly how another model works, and for a novice it would be far too frustrating to work out. Check that all the hand tools mentioned in the manual are still with the machine.

New machines

Choosing a new knitting machine isn't easy, even if you have plenty of money. Buying the most expensive doesn't guarantee the best machine; and even if it was as simple as that, the most expensive in one place may be cheaper than others elsewhere. Knitting machine retailers sell machines at various discounts. You can find the suppliers from advertisements in *Worldwide Machine Knitting* magazine and other publications dealing with needlecrafts. Many new knitting centres are opening at the moment and competition for customers is keen.

It's just as well to forget about price for the moment and concentrate on the best machine for you. I think that an automatic punchcard machine is the one you're most likely to be happy with – unless you can afford an electronic.

Take the single bed machine to which you can add a ribber. These are the ones usually demonstrated.

What you need to know is which machine is best for you. This means that you should have a demonstration of all the machines you can find, even if you have to travel some distance for the privilege. Each machine has something to offer which the others don't – and that something may be very important to you. Comparing machines is hard work, it takes time and energy, and you won't get much help. However, you don't want to spend a great deal of money on something that doesn't suit you particularly well, only to find that just the right machine was there all along.

One source of information might be the local authority evening classes which are organised in many areas. I once went to a tailoring course, and there were six or seven different makes and models of sewing machines for people to use. That's how I found out which sewing machine to buy; I had the chance to try them all, and, equipped with the information and experience, was able to ask all the right questions at the shops. I got the right machine for me.

Talk to any machine knitters you know; but remember, they may well be prejudiced in favour of their own machines. Very likely they won't know any others. So, read – talk – look; try out, if you can. Don't be rushed. *You're* going to be the one who uses the machine. Stay flexible. Be on the look-out for an even better machine. One day you may change that latest model, or even want a second one.

Room for knitting
The place

Finding the right place to knit in can be rather difficult to work out and I think it's worth giving it some thought. If you have a spare room, that's ideal. I like to work in rather a mess; it gives me a feeling of creating out of chaos. If you're tidy, so

much the better for everyone else. There's no point in putting your machine away every time you finish with it. It takes quite a while to set up and put away, and if you have to set it up whenever you want to knit you certainly won't make use of a spare ten minutes.

Perhaps the most important thing about any place you choose is the light. Daylight is very much better than artificial. Dark colours can be very tiring to work with in artificial light. But if you're using artificial light the best is fluorescent tubing, which doesn't cast dark shadows.

Some knitting takes concentration. If you haven't got a punchcard machine any stitch pattern you use will need a certain concentration. Even with a punchcard machine you may choose to do some of the patterning semi-automatically. This sort of knitting needs a place where you and the machine won't be disturbed.

In any case you'll find you get interrupted while you're knitting. It's bad enough to leave a piece of knitting on the machine for any length of time, as it tends to get distorted, but it's hopeless if you have to keep on restarting. So find a quiet corner if you can't find a room, and make a cover to go over the machine on its table. If you don't have a cover you'll not only get dust – people may play about with your machine. It's not unknown for a 'friend' to casually push the carriage across without any yarn . . . and that piece of knitting comes off the needles. So make sure you give it the private, hands-off look. You'll have to do better than that for pets, of course – and children. I'm sure you can figure it out, but figure it out you must.

Another point is often overlooked. The machines are noisy to use. You won't be popular if you're knitting in the TV room. A bedroom can be a good place. If yours isn't all that warm in winter, try keeping a small electric heater near the machine and put it on to begin with if you're cold. Machine knitting is actually quite warm work, so once you're started you won't need much heat, but you will need some to keep your hands warm and supple.

If you have to keep an eye on the children, you'll need to be near them, probably downstairs. Perhaps the dining room has a spare corner. Even in a large kitchen you get bits of food near the machine, so I wouldn't use that except as a last resort.

Storing yarn You'll find that you accumulate rather a lot of yarn in no time at all; it seems to grow. I use black plastic dustbin bags to store mine. Transparent ones might be better – I could see what I've

A place for tools You'll use a number of hand tools when using your machine. The tool tray supplied with my machine is useless because it's flat and shallow. What is needed is a set of containers which can easily take the long, thinnish objects which most of the tools are. An ideal holder is a plastic container with several sections, designed to hold pencils and pens and stationery items for a desk top. (See figure 60.)

Looking after the machine You should get used to cleaning and oiling the machine regularly, as otherwise it won't work properly. The instruction manuals tell you how to do this. On many machines you also need to look at the brushes under the carriage quite often. Twirl them round; if they don't move easily, it will be because bits of yarn and fluff have got caught under them. This is where a star-headed screw-driver is useful. You'll need a reasonably large one to get good leverage. Undo the screw which holds each brush in place, and take it and its washer off. Now lift off the brush, remove the fluff and yarn, clean it with a tissue if it's dusty, and then put it back and screw it down as it was before. It's best to do each one in turn – there are two ways of putting back the brushes on my machine and I need the others in place to show me how it should be done. It's not at all difficult to do, and, like any other mechanical adjustments your machine needs from time to time, it's best done by the knitter rather than relying on someone else. You don't want to bother to wait for someone to help you when you're in the middle of a garment. (See figure 61.)

You may also have to change a needle sometimes. Actually I've only had to do this once, but some people have to do it quite often. Again, the instructions for this are in your manual, and it's easy to do. I've never had to have a machine serviced.

What to wear One last, rather obvious, point. Do remember not to wear long, floppy sleeves, particularly knitted ones. Loose threads or materials can easily catch in the needles and either the needle gets bent or your garment gets snagged or both. Wear tight cuffs or roll your sleeves up. Large costume jewellery is also best left off.

Learning to machine knit

So you've decided to buy a knitting machine, you've looked at several, and you've found the right one.

Figure 60 *Knitting machine tools in a convenient holder*

got – but I bought the black ones in bulk, so now I'm stuck with those. There's no weight problem, they keep out the dust, and they can be pushed into cupboards when visitors are due.

You could label them, if you're methodical. I don't think it's worth it – the contents keep changing, and I've got a good memory for things that interest me. Mothballs come in very handy, as they keep mice as well as moths away.

Figure 61 *Brush unscrewed from underneath a sinker arm assembly. Pieces of yarn and fluff can now be removed, and the brush put back before the next one is taken off*

Lessons at the shop Maybe you'll be offered a course of free lessons with your machine; one often is. By all means take it, if it doesn't involve you in too much travelling. The lessons are often rather public, in the shop, and interrupted by customers buying odds and ends.

Postal course You may have been offered a postal course. It's certainly worth trying if you like learning in that way. It's probably free, so you don't lose anything by doing it.

Learning from a friend Maybe you know a machine knitter who's willing to help. Well, it's a very generous offer, so accept it – if you don't think it will wreck your relationship.

Other knitters are often very generous; but they may use a different machine, have a different purpose in mind, only use acrylic yarns; there may be any number of reasons why their knowledge is of limited use to you.

Local authority classes or schools Local authority or other classes can be very useful, but there's one thing you have to bear in mind with all forms of teaching: the teacher is just one person with one outlook. I like to get my teaching from as many sources as possible. So I talk about the subject to as many well informed people as I can. And I get hold of as many books as I can. Each book will have something to offer – even if it's only one helpful sentence.

Teaching yourself You can teach yourself quite easily. First of all set up your machine; read the instruction book very carefully. It's usually translated from the Japanese and very quaint, but, if you re-read the sentences that puzzle you several times, eventually the meaning will be clear. The book will tell you the basic functions of the machine you have, but not much else.

It won't even really tell you what part of the machine does what. It will tell you what the result of a certain action on your part and on the part of the machine will be, but often it won't tell you why. That's what you need to know if you're to get the most out of your machine.

The only way to find that out is by trial and error. Play with your machine; don't worry about making anything unless you want to. It's the playing that will do the teaching, so don't grudge the time it takes. Ignore people who say 'Now you've spent so much, what about getting some saving done?' First you need to thoroughly know your machine, and, if you like playing, just play and enjoy it. You bought it to enjoy. Don't feel guilty!

If you're making something, don't be too rigid about what it is to be. That sounds contradictory, I know. But suppose you're making a simple jumper with rectangular, unshaped sleeves – a very good idea for a first attempt at a garment. If you're wise you'll start with the sleeves. Suppose they get a bit too long – why not turn them into a scarf? Maybe you really need a scarf, anyway. Be adaptable; it's amazing what can turn up. If there's a cuff at the end it will make it simpler to invent an unusual finish or turn it into a shrug. Just add another cuff at the other end. Maybe there are no cuffs; then you can finish off with fringing, make a cushion cover or even place-mats.

The main thing to bear in mind is that it's you who's going to use the machine; don't let the machine use you. It's you who's going to have to do the work of learning – do it your way.

When you're learning, you'll come across snags. A few snags solved by yourself will give you confidence; confidence will mean you'll feel sure you can overcome future snags. There'll always be new problems, because you'll be pushing ahead. You'll be doing things no one else has done. That's the fun of it.

How long will it take? At one time, one advertising leaflet said you could learn to machine knit in five minutes. I think it meant that you can learn to thread up the yarn and push the carriage across in that time, which is probably true. Knitmaster offer a few hours' tuition with their machines. You'll learn a fair amount in that time. The main thing is to get used to the 'feel' of the machine – to allow yourself time to absorb the basic knitting actions so that they become second nature. When you can push the carriage across easily, without feeling any tension or anxiety, you'll know how to machine knit. Don't worry if it seems to take a long time to get to this stage. Once you've absorbed the basic method, you'll go on learning, and the mastering of each technique will make the next that much easier to learn.

Where do I find patterns? All the patterns in this book are simple enough for beginners to hand or machine knit. You can use any of them and Chapter 6 will explain the very simplest garment pattern in detail. You can also buy plenty of other patterns for machine knitting. The local newsagent will stock magazines for knitters and the yarn shop will have some patterns especially written for machine knitters and widely available. Some of the yarn suppliers also supply patterns, so if you're sending off for yarn you can send for the patterns at the same time.

Apart from patterns especially written for machine knitters, it's not particularly difficult to adapt many of the hand knitting patterns. Just avoid the ones which shape within rows rather than at the edges of a garment piece, those using more stitches than there are needles on your machine, and those using special hand stitch patterns. You'll have to find the tension on the machine which corresponds to the needle size, and you may have to adjust the number of rows to the centimetre or inch. But as long as you get the number of stitches to the unit right, you can adjust the length without too much trouble.

Best of all, design your own patterns. Chapter 6 should get you started.

5 THE VITAL THREAD

The finest tools and the greatest skills are of little use if the raw materials are inadequate. The raw materials for the crafts of hand and machine knitting and crochet are yarns, particularly knitting yarns. A few other long, thin, flexible objects like leather thongs and ribbons can also be used successfully.

It's important to realise what yarn is: it is by no means obvious. For example, many people think of yarn as synonymous with wool. But I hope to show them that it's not; though the word wool is used to mean yarn made of wool fibre, yarn isn't necessarily wool. The raw materials of yarn are textile fibres of various kinds. Fibres come in two forms: as 'staples' (or short lengths) and as 'filaments' (or long lengths). Knitting yarn is primarily produced from staple fibres, or filament fibres cut into staple lengths. It can briefly be described as an elongated piece of twisted or spun material, consisting of one or more threads, strands or plies, whatever the fibre content, the method of spinning, the thickness, or the quality.

Many patterns tell you which yarn to use, and, for the most part, that particular yarn will work well enough for that particular pattern. But a particular yarn is often suggested because the pattern has been published by the firm which manufactures the yarn. It's in their interests to suggest that only that yarn should be used; it's in your interests to decide whether or not they're right.

Some people feel that only yarn made of natural fibres is worth crafting with at all; I think this is a very big mistake. While I feel strongly that all that is handed down traditionally should be preserved if it contributes to our present creative processes, I feel equally strongly that anything new which can add to these same processes should be seized on with enthusiasm, and made part of the heritage. Natural fibres have many fine attributes; this statement in no way detracts from the equally fine attributes of so many man-made fibres. The purpose of this chapter is to give a very brief guide to the many beautiful yarns which are now available, to suggest the most appropriate use for each yarn, and to give an idea of

Figure 62 *The Woolmark (Courtesy International Wool Secretariat)*

the advantages and disadvantages of each yarn so far as hand and machine knitting are concerned.

Quality

Quality, above all, is very important to anyone taking the trouble to craft rather than to mass produce articles. But quality is not easily defined. A good example is given by the attempt to classify wool into qualities. The International Wool Secretariat has introduced the Woolmark. (See figure 62.) As you can see, the phrase Pure New Wool is written under the Woolmark. This indicates that the yarn or article is made of pure wool fibre which hasn't been used in a manufactured product before. However, this isn't sufficient proof of quality. Pure new wool ranges from the sturdiest semi-wild Herdwick wool (said to have been used for John Peel's 'coat so grey') to the softest pure Merino wool. Herdwick may be the best choice for a riding sweater, but Merino will be better for a baby's matinée coat. In other words, the choice must be an appropriate one. The Woolmark takes account of the performance of articles on which it's bestowed, and this includes, as well as fibre content, properties such as colour fastness to light and to washing, shrinkage, and abrasion resistance. In other words, as far as that particular type of knitting wool is concerned, the Woolmark is intended to ensure that the wool is of high enough quality for the knitter's purposes.

In order to make your own choice of quality, you will have to bear all these and other factors in mind. And it isn't as simple as choosing the most expensive yarn, or yarns made of natural fibres only, or of a particular thickness. Fitness for purpose is part of it, appearance is another and, for most of us, cost is yet another.

Types of fibres available as knitting yarns
Natural fibres

Wool Yarn made of wool fibre is very important for knitters, but it isn't the only suitable yarn, and surprisingly often it's not even the best yarn. Wool is, however, a most important type of yarn. There are a number of different fibres which are often loosely termed 'wool'. These are the hairs of several mammals, from the Angora rabbit to the Kashmir goat. But it's the fleece of the domestic sheep which produces the most important wool.

The importance of sheep wool lies in its elasticity and its warmth. The crimp or curl in the fibre holds pockets of air which gives this wool its remarkable insulating quality. It can also be quite moist without feeling damp to the skin – an important factor in cold, damp climates. Though not as strong as many other readily available fibres, its elasticity makes it easy to knit without breaking on a machine, and it's very resilient, giving it excellent wearing properties.

Wool, however has several disadvantages. Worn next to the skin, it can be scratchy. More important it shrinks and felts. The fibres are built up in a scaly fashion; when rubbed in heat or moisture these scales open and connect with the scales of the other fibres near them, matting into a tangled mass. This process is irreversible, but can be delayed by careful handling when washing – though some wools are treated to resist felting, as explained later on. Also moths are fond of wool, it takes a long time to dry after washing, and pilling – little balls of fluff forming on the surface of a fabric – can be a nuisance.

A distinction is often made between two groups of fibres: Merino and Crossbred. Merino comes from the fleece of the Merino sheep, and is often called Botany. It's a fine, soft fibre which can be spun into an even, smooth and delicate yarn. Crossbred wool is loosely used to describe wool from other breeds, and includes pure English and other breeds as well as crossbreeds. These are coarser, springier wools with greater resistance to hard outdoor wear.

Wool quality is influenced by many things other than its fibre: the breed of sheep, the climate where it lives, the food available there, the stage of life it was shorn at, the way the fibre is turned into yarn – even the way it's used for crafting.

Shetland wool comes from Shetland sheep, one of the oldest breeds in the world. The natural fleece colours vary from off white, through shades of brown and red to black, and can be used undyed for traditional fairisle knitting. It can also be spun into a very fine 1-ply, and is used in this form to make the gossamer Shetland shawls. Oiled, cone-wound yarn is used industrially to make articles washed after knitting. This yarn is now available to the domestic knitter, and there is a good choice available.

Shetland wool is often spun very loosely, sometimes having only two strands of thick wool to make a heavy weight yarn. The yarn hasn't as much tensile strength as some other wool yarns, and in consequence care is needed when knitting on a machine, otherwise the yarn will break.

Lambswool is the wool taken from an animal up to eight months old. It's finer and softer than wool shorn from older sheep, whatever the breed, and again is used industrially containing the spinning oil and wound on a cone. This type of yarn is available in a fine – that is a very thin – form to domestic knitters. Again, it needs care when used for knitting by machine, and a slow, steady pace is best.

Superwash wool Some wool is specially treated to make it machine washable without the risk of felting or shrinking. This sort of wool is very easy to knit on a machine, but care is needed in the sewing up. As it has been specially treated to resist felting, the fibres don't cling like other wool fibres and so any knotted yarn ends tend to work loose. All the joins must

Figure 63 *Two undyed shades of alpaca yarn*

therefore be at the ends of rows because the knots come undone so easily, and care is needed to fasten off properly when making up. This treated wool isn't as elastic as untreated; ribbed welts don't have that lasting cling which is such a feature of untreated wool. Nevertheless, if you have a lot of knitwear to wash, you may consider that using this treated wool for your knitted clothes is a most helpful technical innovation.

Alpaca Alpaca fibres come from two different breeds of llama, an animal which looks like a small camel without a hump. The fibre is long stapled and very soft, fine and lustrous. It's often mixed with other fibres to make yarn. Alpaca fibres vary considerably in natural colour and, as the fibre is very hard to bleach, the yarn made from it is often sold undyed. The colours vary from the lightest off white to quite a dark charcoal, with greys and beige tones between. I've found it a very hard-wearing yarn, but inclined to be scratchy, even when worn over other clothes. The fine fibres seem to find their way through any fabric. It's a slippery yarn, which makes it very easy to knit on a knitting machine. Again, care has to be taken in making up and joining in new ends, as knots easily come undone. (See figure 63.)

Angora Angora fibres come from the hair of the Angora rabbit. This is a very expensive fibre and is usually mixed with sheep's wool to make yarn. It's particularly soft, very fuzzy, and knits up easily both by hand and machine. The fibre is very warm and light, but, as it's so expensive, the yarn is often used only for the trimmings and edges of a garment. I've used it very successfully on a knitting machine as well as for hand knitting. To bring out the full beauty of the long fibres it should be knitted on a reasonably loose tension. A light brushing with a teazel brush will show off the long fibres after machine knitting, which has a tendency to flatten them. Any garment made of angora should be shaken after washing and allowed to dry in a warm atmosphere to restore its full fluffiness. Figure 64 shows part of a blouse knitted on a basic machine.

Cashmere This is the hair of the Kashmir goat and is even more expensive than the fibres from the Angora rabbit. It's a beautifully fine and warm fibre, and much prized for classical garments. The colours are often soft browns and greys. When bought on the cone the yarn is still oiled, and it has to be knitted at a very loose tension to allow it to expand when the oil has been washed out. The pieces can be washed and brushed after knitting, so that the hairs are matted together to give the traditional

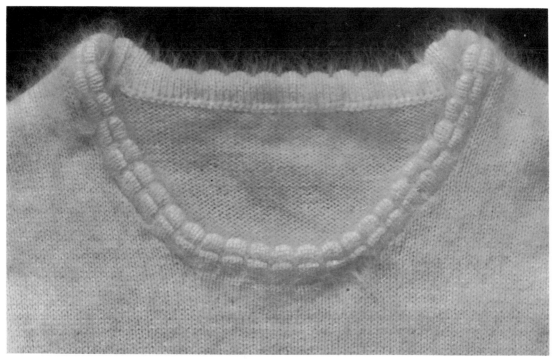

Figure 64 *Angora fibres showing up against a black background. The U-neckline was made by using the holding position, the patterned neckband knitted on after the shaping had been completed*

lightweight and very warm garment.

Mohair Mohair is the name given to the hair of the Angora goat. This has also become a very expensive fibre and is more often than not mixed with wool as well as synthetic fibres. Mohair has a very long staple and fine lustre. The brushed yarn shows up beautifully in hand knitting, and can be used economically and attractively as a weaving yarn for knitweave. Machine knitting tends to flatten the fibres, and this fabric, even when worked with a teazel brush afterwards, doesn't show as good a result as hand knitting. It helps to use a loose tension and a reverse stocking stitch fabric. One of the big advantages of mohair is that it gives greater warmth than wool for less weight. It doesn't shrink or felt as much as wool, and is very long-lasting. Again, it's a fairly scratchy fibre, hard to wear next to the skin. Plate 5 (facing p. 96) shows a garment knitted on every third needle of a basic machine.

Silk Silk is also an animal fibre, but it's not made of hair. It's produced by the silkworm, the caterpillar of the silkmoth, which weaves a cocoon round itself, spinning hundreds of metres (yards) of silk. There are several kinds of silkmoth, and each kind produces a different type of silk. Silk can be processed in two different ways – by reeling straight from the cocoon, and by spinning raw silk waste which isn't reelable. Spun silk is very much cheaper, and the type most often used for knitting. Most silk is produced by the mulberry-feeding silkworm reared specially for the purpose. Cultivated silk is easily dyed to beautiful colours, but it is very expensive.

Tusser or *Tussah silk* is collected from the wild and is much coarser than that of the mulberry-feeding silkworm. The natural colour is a tan or brown from the tannin in the oak leaves on which this silkworm feeds. It's not easy to bleach this fibre, so that it's often sold in its natural colour. This silk is much cheaper, but still produces a beautiful yarn, often of a knobbly or slub texture.

Silk is smooth, lustrous, warm and reasonably elastic. Though not as warm as wool, it's a very strong yarn and has a luxurious feel. Knitting it isn't at all difficult, and garments made of silk are well worthwhile.

Cotton Cotton is another natural fibre, obtained from the hairs on the seed pod of a plant of the Mallow family. Cotton is easy to spin because of the

Figure 65 *A skirt knitted in a slip stitch pattern, using a slub cotton yarn*

rising process, and then shrinkage is reduced to a minimum. This yarn isn't as easy to knit by machine as wool because it's not as elastic. It's as well to acquire a certain skill in machine knitting before using cotton. It's popular for crochet for this reason. However, the knitted fabric is itself elastic, and very attractive clothes can be made by knitting the yarn. The 'hang' for a skirt is particularly good. (See figure 65.)

Linen Another well-known plant fibre is flax. Linen is made from the fibre in the stalks of the flax plant. It makes a very strong but inelastic yarn. The processes by which the fibres are turned into yarn are fairly expensive, so it's not widely available for knitting. To reduce the expense the yarn is often supplied mixed with cotton or synthetic fibres. Knitting with it is comparable to knitting with cotton. Garments made from it are very useful for summer wear, very long-lasting, and easily washed. But they do crease.

Man-made fibres

Man-made fibres come in two forms – the regenerated fibres produced from cellulose, like the various rayons, and the synthetic fibres, that is those made by man from rather unlikely raw materials like coal tar, water, petroleum and so on.

Rayon

Viscose rayon is made from cellulose, like cotton linters or wood pulp. It has about half the strength of silk and is particularly vulnerable when wet, so that care has to be taken when laundering it. There's greater elasticity than in cotton or linen, though not as much as in wool or silk. The result is that the articles made from it may sag, and this point needs to be borne in mind when knitting; a firm stitch pattern is useful for skirts, for instance. Viscose is a good conductor of heat and makes good summer wear. The smoothness of the fibres makes it shed dirt easily. It does shrink, however, even more than cotton, and knitted fabrics are particularly liable to this because of the loose construction. Dye is absorbed evenly, and the slightly silky lustre combines well with other yarns to make interesting fabrics. It's essential to consider the effect washing or other treatments will have on the combined yarns before planning a garment. Viscose is resistant to moths but may mildew if left damp.

Cuprammonium rayon is slightly less elastic than viscose rayon, and less absorbent. It also tends to

natural twist in the fibre. It makes strong, fine yarns though they're by no means as elastic as wool. However, it's a pleasant material to wear, especially in hot weather when it soaks up perspiration and keeps the wearer comfortable. Cotton becomes stronger when wet and doesn't felt, so it's easy to wash.

Mercerised cotton Yarns are often sold which have had a special treatment called mercerisation given to the fibres, which increases the strength and lustre of the fibre, and makes it easier to dye.

One disadvantage of cotton is that it shrinks considerably. Some yarns are treated by the sanfo-

shrink, but can be made shrink resistant. The lustre of the yarn is more subdued than viscose but there's still a silklike appearance and feel.

Acetate rayon differs from rayon in that the fibres aren't pure cellulose, but have chemical compounds added and so have their own special properties. The fibres aren't as strong as other rayon fibres and have relatively poor abrasion resistance; consequently they're not as hard-wearing. Acetate is, however, more elastic than other rayons and fairly resilient, so that yarns will return to their original shape. But it isn't as absorbent as other rayons. Garments made of it tend to feel clammy in humid weather – though they have the advantage of drying quickly.

The smoothness of the fibres makes it shed dirt easily, though it's not as strong when wet as it is when dry and therefore needs careful handling when it's being washed. There's less shrinkage than with other rayons and it's resistant to both mildew and moths. Dyeing acetate isn't easy as it's not very absorbent, and so is unsuitable for home dyeing.

Nylon The word nylon is used to describe a textile, like cotton or wool. Trade names include Bri-nylon, Wellon, Enkalen.

Nylon knitting yarns are made from staple lengths spun, usually, on the cotton system. Compared to wool, these yarns are very strong, and care has to be taken when machine knitting – a piece of yarn caught on a needle or in part of the machine mechanism can cause damage because it doesn't break as wool does.

Nylon is usually thought of as shrink-resistant and easily washable, but this is only true of properly heat set fibres. It's possible to buy industrially coned yarns which are *not* heat set and which will shrink quite considerably, and this has to be borne in mind when buying and using coned nylon yarn.

The fibre doesn't absorb much moisture, and it's not particularly useful for humid conditions. There is also a certain tendency to pill. Washing should therefore be reasonably gentle. The yarn also has a low melting point – great care must be used when pressing. The transparent nylon threads often used for punch lace knitting can now be bought in heat resistant form.

The great advantage of nylon is its strength; it makes a very good fibre to add to wool to produce yarns for socks and other articles which get rough wear. There's no difficulty with mildew or moths.

Polyesters These fibres are produced from ele-

ments derived from coal tar, water and petroleum. Trade names include Terylene, Dacron, Kodel.

Again, knitting yarns are made from staple lengths spun on the cotton or wool systems, and these fibres, too, need to be stabilised by heat setting so that they don't shrink.

The fibres in this group are relatively strong, but not as strong as nylon. Yarns made from them are particularly easy to use for machine knitting, as they're smooth and elastic. They also have the advantage of being highly resilient, and are warmer then yarns made of cotton, linen or rayon. They're absolutely resistant to mildew and moths. Moreover, they're very easy to wash and dry, and can be pressed at the temperature used for rayon.

The disadvantages of polyester fibres are that they're the least absorbent of those discussed so far, so they're clammy and uncomfortable to wear in humid weather. Home dyeing isn't possible as specialised techniques have to be used.

Acrylics Acrylic fibres are made from a type of plastic; trade names include Orlon and Acrylan. As with polyesters, staple yarns are spun on the cotton or wool systems and are made into fuzzy yarns. High bulk yarns can be made by crimping the staple before it's spun, and thick, soft, spongy yarns can be produced which will make up into warm, lightweight garments with a reasonably luxurious feel. The yarns are stronger than wool, though not as strong as other natural fibres. They wear well but there's little elasticity. Knitted in a firm stitch pattern, the garments don't pull out of shape; but loosely knitted garments do tend to lose their shape easily. These yarns are very easy to use for machine knitting, and are often recommended for beginners.

Acrylics don't conduct heat rapidly and so can be reasonably warm to wear. These yarns dry slowly in comparison with the polyesters and nylons. Absorbency is low, so their insulating quality can be as good as wool, though they'll feel cold in a damp climate. Again, they need proper processing before they're shrink resistant, but once processed will not shrink much. There's a tendency to pill and care is needed when ironing. Mildew can affect the surface, but will not affect the fabric. The fibre is moth-proof and can be home dyed quite easily.

Chlorofibre This is a synthetic fibre used with acrylic fibre to make thermacryl, a yarn rivalling the warmth of wool. Though I don't find it quite as warm, it certainly has some advantages over wool for a number of purposes: it's very smooth and silky

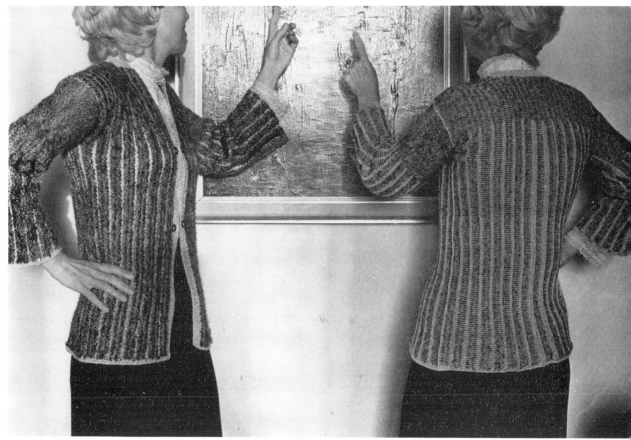

Figure 66 *Two garments for the work of one. The knitted base is worked in a thin lurex yarn strengthened with transparent nylon thread. The weaving yarn is a random flecked acrylic poodle*

and consequently easy to wear next to the skin – made up in underwear, for example – it doesn't felt or pill, it dries quickly, and it's machine washable. Machine washable wool has to be washed on a special programme on the machine, whereas chlorófibre can be washed at a low temperature setting, like any of the synthetics. Chlorofibre must be dried away from direct heat and cannot be pressed or steamed. I've found only one supplier of therm-acrylic yarn, who supplies it in a medium thickness and only in white. The yarn knits easily, both by hand and machine. (See figure 4.)

Metal threads and tinsel Some very interesting metallic yarns can be made by sandwiching metal, usually aluminium foil, between two layers of clear polyester film. This produces a silver yarn. Other colours can also be made.

These metallic yarns can be made very flexible and combined with other fibres in various ways to give splendid yarns with exciting potential. However, as they're made of plastic covered films they're liable to melt in the same way as the other plastic yarns, and must be treated with care when they're ironed or subjected to other forms of heat. Trade names include Lurex, Melton and Durastron.

These yarns are particularly attractive when twisted with other textile fibres, or 'run in' with other yarns during the knitting. There's nothing particularly difficult about using them, though they do have very low tensile strength and I've sometimes found it necessary to run in a transparent nylon thread with a thin metallic mixture yarn so that it doesn't break when machine knitting. (See fig. 66.)

Mixed fibre yarns Some of the most successful modern yarns are made of fibre mixtures. This often means that the advantages of many fibres are combined, and their disadvantages minimised.

A section on suppliers has been compiled to help

71

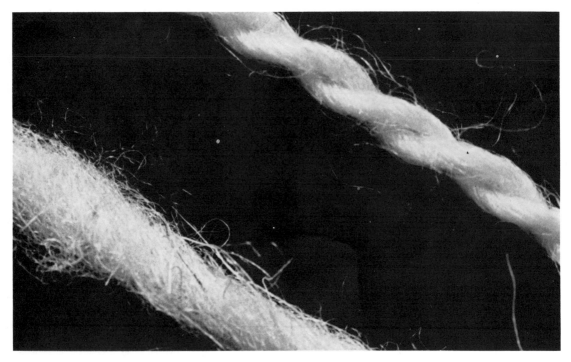

Figure 67 *Worsted yarn in the top right hand corner, woollen yarn in the bottom left hand corner*

you find unusual yarns, and can be found at the end of the book.

Spinning

The fibres from which the yarn is made aren't the only things that matter. The yarn has to be spun – the fibres twisted together in some way to make them cling to each other and, in the case of the relatively short stapled fibres from which most knitting yarn is made, to produce a piece of thread of appropriate length.

Before staple fibres are spun, two different processes are used which will give quite different yarns. For yarns made of wool fibre, these different processes produce *worsted* or *woollen* yarns. For other fibres, the yarns are said to be spun on the worsted or woollen systems.

Worsted yarn Wool fibre comes in different lengths, or staples, some of which are reasonably long. The longer stapled fibres are separated from any broken or short ones and laid as nearly parallel to one another as possible. Longer fibres will make a stonger yarn because there's greater adhesion – the number of twists along any given fibre length will be

greater and help it to cling more firmly to the other fibres. (See figure 67.) The result will be a smooth, strong yarn able to take hard wear.

Woollen yarn Short stapled fibres can be used for this way of preparing yarn. The fibres are first laid parallel, and then deliberately and evenly tangled before spinning. The result is a fuzzy yarn, with a number of fibre ends sticking out, which isn't as strong as worsted but has the advantage of greater warmth for less weight. (See figure 67.) The *quality* of the yarn depends on a number of factors; a woollen yarn may come from exactly the same source as a worsted yarn, using, for instance, the broken ends of fibre. However, it can often be produced more cheaply.

Direction of twist Obviously there are two ways of twisting: clockwise and anti-clockwise. You can see for yourself which way a yarn has been twisted by trying to untwist it; if you turn it clockwise and it gets tighter and shorter, you know it's been twisted in that direction, and vice versa.

Amount of twist Quite apart from the direction, there's going to be a definite amount of twist. Generally there are four categories:

(1) Soft twist yarns, like the Icelandic and Shet-

Plate 1 *Fairisle sweater made to Pattern 1. Knitted in an oatmeal Shetland wool, with the pattern worked in a doubled fine mohair yarn in green and gold*

Plate 2 *Yoked knitwoven jacket made to Pattern 2. The base yarn is a fine blue acrylic, the weaving yarn a toning random acrylic poodle*

Plate 4 *All-over fairisle jumper made to Pattern 4. The jumper was knitted in a 4-ply superwash wool using two shades of red*

Plate 3 *Reversible raglan jacket made to Pattern 3 on the right, duffle coat adapted from Pattern 1 on the left. The raglan is knitted in an oatmeal Shetland wool combined with a beige acrylic bouclé. The duffle is knitwoven in a fawn superwash wool combined with a pink slub yarn*

land yarns. The very soft Icelandic type of wool, for instance, has little twist and hand knitting adds just enough to make it sufficiently strong for a garment. It's too delicate for machine knitting.

(2) Medium twist yarns, like the well-known 'knitting' yarns, are the most common for hand or machine knitting.

(3) Hard twist yarns, like many worsted yarns, used for socks and guernseys, for instance.

(4) Very hard twist yarns, like crêpe yarns, which give a very hard-wearing fabric and make it easy for inexperienced hand knitters to produce an even fabric. Figure 68 shows an example of each type.

Plies, strands and folds The spinning process produces a single thread, called a strand, ply or fold. Combining several strands leads to the well-known names used for hand knitting yarns. One-ply yarn is rarely used now, but was traditionally used to make Shetland wedding shawls. They were so fine that they could be threaded through a wedding ring. More often, knitters use 2-, 3- or 4-ply yarns, and other groupings called double knitting, quicker knit, triple knitting and so on.

It is, of course, possible to produce any particular

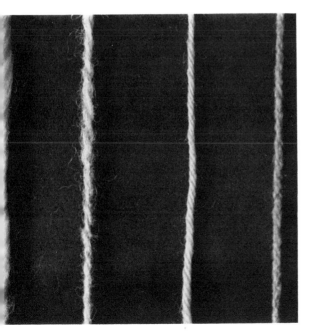

Figure 68 *From left to right: a soft twist yarn, a medium twist yarn, a hard twist yarn, and a very hard twist yarn*

thickness in 1-ply. However, a 'singles' yarn may be of perfectly good quality and still not quite strong enough for a particular purpose. Where durability is important, it's useful to twist singles yarns together — to ply them. It makes it easy to control the thickness, by choosing how many plies of a particular thickness of strand to combine. The yarn is twisted again, and here the direction of the twist can be significant. *Plying*, that is twisting yarns in an anticlockwise direction which have previously been twisted clockwise will make softer yarns than *cabling*, which is twisting yarns still further in the direction of their original twist. Plying will add strength without hardness, cabling will add greater strength but will result in a tougher yarn, not always suitable for knitting.

Doubled yarns Another method is to combine several strands without twisting them in any way. These yarns are known as *doubled yarns*, however many strands are used. This method doesn't have the same effect as a plied yarn, but it's useful to the modern machine knitter and the maxi knitter. A number of fine, industrially coned yarns can be bought and 'run in' together by taking several ends from a number of cones or wound balls. These won't make yarns identical to the plied yarns of the same thickness, but they do give great creative scope in combining one's own fine-strand yarns.

Oiled yarn Before natural fibres can be spun they have to be put through several processes. These take out the natural oils in wool fibres, and in order to make them smooth and strong enough to spin, they need to have oil added back to them. Knitting yarns sold in shops have had this oil removed; industrial yarns, sold on the cone, often have this oil still on the yarns.

Some people like to wear oiled wool garments; these are fairly waterproof, especially if knitted on a tight tension. Most people, however, wash the garment pieces after knitting. It's important to know that when the oil is washed out the fibres expand; for this reason oily yarns must be knitted at a looser tension than scoured or cleaned yarns. It's *essential* to test the tension swatch by washing it.

The oil often has a distinctive odour; if you're sensitive to odours, you may not enjoy working with oiled yarn. The knitting itself isn't difficult, because the oil acts as a lubricant.

Yarn count Hand knitters are used to thinking of yarn weights in terms of ply or other names. This

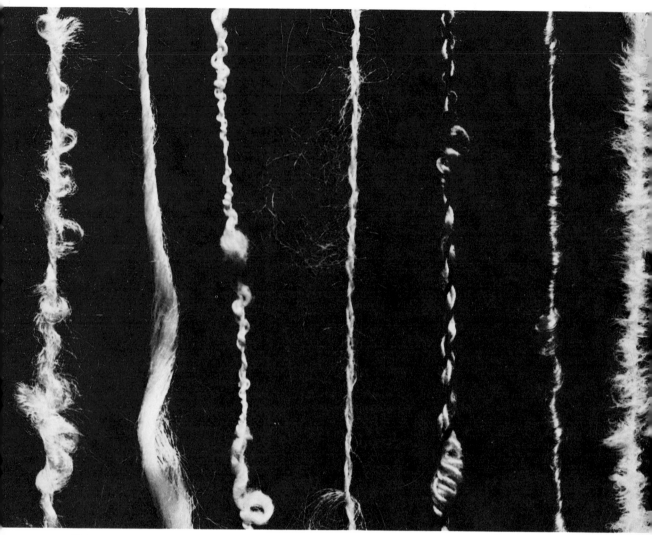

Figure 69 *From left to right: loop, slub, bouclé, brushed, fancy nub, spiral and chenille yarns*

isn't an accurate way of describing the yarn thickness, as it depends not only on the thickness of the original strand, which varies considerably, but also on the amount of twist and the method of plying. In industry it's necessary to have a more exact description, and yarn thicknesses are expressed in terms of linear units relative to units of weight, often given in yards per pound or metres per kilogram. The number of folds is given separately.

Several systems are used. The 'count' system used in English speaking countries isn't universal even in that restricted area; it depends on the system used by a particular mill for particular fibres, and this can

vary from mill to mill. A greatly simplified explanation of the count system is this: two numbers are given, the first separated from the second by a stroke, for instance 2/14. What it means is that the first number gives the number of folds, strands or plies twisted together to make the yarn. The second number, called the count number, gives the unit of length to the unit of weight which the mill uses for this particular fibre. A standard count for cotton is 840 yards to 1 lb of fibre; this is known as number 1 count. Number 2 count would be 1680 yards to 1 lb of fibre, number 50 4200 yards to 1 lb of fibre. The *higher* the count number, the *thinner* the strand.

The fold number gives the number of strands of this thickness put together. A 2/50s cotton will therefore be roughly twice as thick as a 1/50s, the slight difference being dependent on how the yarn was plied or cabled. So the *higher* the fold number, the *thicker* the yarn of a particular strand count.

There are systems for worsted wool, the standard being 560 yards to the pound. Common standards for woollen count are 1600 yards per lb in the US, 256 yards per lb in England, 300 yards per lb in Scotland.

The metric count system is based on a fixed length of 1000 metres for all fibres – the count number is the number of 1000 metre lengths in each kilo. In this system the fold number usually follows the count number.

Deniers are used to describe the silk and synthetic filament yarns. The denier number gives the weight in grammes of 9000 metres of yarn – the greater the number, the *thicker* the yarn.

A new international system, called Tex, has been introduced but isn't yet in general use. The Tex number gives the weight in grammes of 1000 metres of yarn. Again, the greater the Tex number, the thicker the yarn.

A singles yarn giving 250 metres to a 25 gm ball, or 315 yards to a 1 oz ball, can be described as roughly equivalent in the following five ways:

Tex	Deniers	Cotton count	Metric count	Worsted count
100	900	6	10	9

When you buy industrially coned yarns you will see the count numbers stuck inside the cone or given in some other way. You can only compare like with like; wool, for instance, has counts for both woollen and worsted yarns, as we have seen. Some suppliers give the length of yarn in a particular weight of ball or cone; this is very helpful for comparing yarns.

Texture

Different ways of spinning can be used to provide texture as well as thickness. Figure 69 shows seven differently textured yarns.

Crêpe yarns have already been mentioned; this is a yarn where the amount of twist is at its maximum without doubling back on itself.

Nub yarns are produced by increasing the twist so that the yarn starts doubling back on itself. This is done at regular intervals along the yarn.

Slub yarns are spun in such a way that they have soft, untwisted pieces along parts of their length,

interrupted by more tightly spun pieces.

Flake yarns show a slub effect; this is produced by twisting a soft spun yarn with harder and often thinner spun yarns.

Spiral yarns have soft thick yarns spun round very hard spun, thin yarn.

Bouclé yarns use the spiral principle, but often have the softer yarn looped back on itself to form random thick pieces along the yarn.

Looped yarns can be a variation of bouclé yarns, where identical yarns are twisted together with one forming loops, the other twisting round to keep the loops in place.

Chenille yarns are made so that fibre ends stick out all along the yarn length, held together by a central core of fine yarn.

Though many of these yarns aren't as hard-wearing as conventionally spun yarn, they're very popular.

Dyeing

The yarns we use depend for their effect not only on their fibre content or texture, but also on their colour.

Colour can be added to yarn either by dyeing the fibre, or by dyeing the yarn. Different fibres need different treatments with different dyestuffs. Even the same fibres are dyed with different dyes because some colours are better produced by one method than another. This can, and does, affect the yarn and consequently the feel of the knitted fabric. It also, as I've stressed in Chapter 6, affects the tension to which the yarn knits up.

Dyeing is a complex subject, but it's useful to know that a few fibres can easily be dyed with natural or readily obtainable chemical dyes. Fibres of all kinds differ in their capacity to take dyestuffs. As fibres vary so much in their make-up, it's easy to see that no one dye will satisfactorily dye all fibres.

With all the very good colours and dyed yarns on the market, it might seem odd to want to dye one's own yarn. However, there are a few limitations to commercially produced yarns. Colours produced by a batch of natural dyes cannot easily be repeated, so for a completely individual colour, in a soft shade, natural materials offer a creative outlet. It's impossible to buy really good dip-dyed yarn because commercial yarns are 'random' dyed in a regular way – a contradiction in terms, of course. Fortunately, dip-dyeing is a particularly easy way to dye one's own yarn, and it won't need perfect matching if you run out and have to dye some more.

Not all fibres can be dyed by home methods, but wool, cotton, viscose, silk and nylon can all give good results.

Skeining yarns Yarns wound on balls or on cones will have to be rewound into skeins or hanks so that the dyestuff can penetrate properly. I've listed one supplier of skeined, undyed knitting yarn in wool and nylon; unfortunately this is only available in one thickness each. The wool yarn still contains oil, and needs to be scoured before dyeing. Other suppliers offer bleached yarns, natural-coloured yarns or white dyed yarns. Each will have a different effect on the dye.

Scouring yarns Scouring is best done by dissolving two tablespoons of washing soda in about two gallons of hand hot water. Squeeze the skeined yarn gently in this for several minutes and then rinse several times; alternatively a mild detergent can be used.

Dylon dyes are readily available if you wish to buy chemical dyes, and the leaflets which come with them explain the methods to use. Natural dyes often have to be combined with a 'mordant' – a chemical added to the dyebath to fasten the dye more securely to the fibres.

Preparing yarns for knitting

You can hand knit with virtually anything in yarn form – that is anything which is long and relatively thin, like ribbons, leather thonging, braids, all kinds of things . . . This doesn't mean it will be successful, but it's all worth a try in the hope of getting individual results. Machine knitting is a little more restrictive, but there is one bonus: you can use much finer yarns than are practical for most hand knitting. If you add knitweave to your repertoire, you can use many of the more exotic yarns, or yarn-like materials, as weaving yarns.

The yarn materials you buy will be wound in some way, but may not be in a form which is suitable for knitting. Yarn must be wound into a ball or other tangle-free form for all knitting methods. Though no special system is needed for hand knitting, the speed of machine knitting means that the prepared yarn must unwind quickly and without obstruction. If you buy yarn on the cone, it's usually ready for

machine knitting without more ado. Occasionally it isn't waxed, and you might have to arrange for it to go through a wax disc as you knit, or to spray it with a special lubricant.

Winding yarn To prepare wound hand knitting yarns for machine knitting, you'll need to wax and rewind them on a winder, as described in Chapter 4. (See figure 59.) The yarn must be rewound so that it *unwinds easily*. In most cases this means guiding it to slip without tension through your fingers as you wind. Don't wind too fast to begin with, otherwise the yarn winds at a tension. Winding two hand knitting balls, one on top of the other, will speed up the work, though you have to be on the lookout for the joining knot when you're doing the actual knitting. Unfortunately yarn can have knots in it apart from that one, whether wound in a ball or in any other way. This is a great nuisance, particularly to the machine knitter. What I do is to make the knot *bigger* so that I cannot fail to notice it as I knit. Then I make sure that I pull the knot to the nearest edge. Of course this wastes a certain amount of yarn. I find it easier to pull the knotted yarn through the yarn brake by hand rather than re-threading yarns, so I always attach my newly wound ball to the old one.

Waxing or lubricating It's important to smooth fuzzy or knobbly yarns for machine knitting. The first waxing is done while rewinding the yarn, if that's necessary. It pays to wax again while knitting. This is easily done by attaching a wax disc to the yarn brake. For those which don't allow for this, you'll have to work out your own method – one which is suited to your machine.

Estimating yarn needs

Yarn is expensive, and you may feel that you should only buy the amount you actually need. I find that, as long as I buy *enough* of a particular dye batch, left-over yarn is never wasted. Properly kept, it stays in good condition for a long time.

Instead of agonising over exact amounts, I always buy my yarn in the standard packs offered by the supplier. For some this is a bulk amount of between 1 to 5 kg (5 to 10 lbs); for others it might be a pack of 20 wound balls. Knitting large size garments in a medium yarn uses roughly that amount. Smaller sizes leave enough yarn to use as contrast in another garment. In this way I've accumulated many textures and colours, and this helps enormously when working out new fabrics. The most unlikely colour combinations can turn out to be the best, and I might never have thought of some of my successful ones if I hadn't had the colours to experiment with.

Weighing garment pieces Once you have your 'yarn store', it's useful to know what you can make with particular amounts. If you weigh each garment *piece* in each of the different yarn thicknesses you use, and write these weights down in a notebook, you'll soon know quite accurately how much you need for a particular project. Working the pieces in the most useful order – body before sleeves, for instance – gives you the chance to adjust the sleeve length to the amount of yarn still available. Halve it, knit from the sleeve head to the cuff, and stop when you get near the end of the yarn allotted for that sleeve, just leaving yourself enough to finish it in whatever way you please.

It's also very useful to weigh any yarn you have left over, and to label it with that weight. Don't forget that the cone itself weighs between 20 and 30 grammes ($\frac{3}{4}$ oz to 1 oz).

Estimating for knitweave The amount of yarn you need for the basic knitted fabric will not differ appreciably from any other knitted fabric. The amount you need for weaving is quite easily estimated by length. The length to weight of yarn is often given by the supplier. For weaving, you need the number of woven rows in a garment piece multiplied by the width of the longest row. This gives sufficient leeway for turning and weaving unless all the rows are of equal length. In that case allow enough to cover this – depending, of course, on the size of the piece.

There's a vast choice of yarns in wool shops, in stores and from mail order suppliers. Don't forget that cotton sewing threads, invisible nylon thread and metallic threads are all types of yarn. They can provide you with the opportunity to make quite new fabrics either by using them with ordinary knitting yarns or by judicious use of the stitch pattern mechanism on many knitting machines.

Some people are so worried by the difficulties of knitting to the right tension that they stick to only one yarn of one thickness and only vary the colour. I think you'd be denying yourself a marvellous creative outlet if you took this attitude. The next chapter will show you how to minimise the tension problems. Using very simple pattern shapes for unisex garments for any age group will give you the confidence to try out all types and thicknesses of yarn. Allow the yarns to make the different fabrics for you; they can do this by their colours, their textures, their fibre contents, their thicknesses. Once you've enjoyed using a large range of yarns you'll be much more self-assured. At that stage you can extend your experiments by combining different stitch patterns as well as different yarns.

6 FIRST CATCH YOUR TENSION

I've stressed the advantages of knitted fabric and the pleasure that comes from creating your own garments and other knitted articles. Now I'd like to show you how to set about making a garment in the simplest way. I shall deal with this in detail because the method I advocate isn't often suggested for hand knitters, though machine knitters who have a charting device will already use it.

Instead of trying to match a particular tension given in a pattern, you make your own fabric in your own choice of yarn and tension. You mark this fabric while you're knitting so that you can measure it later. In this way you'll have no problems about getting the right tension, no problems about measuring it, no need to use a pattern, and you'll have mastered the first step in learning how to design knitwear.

Trying to match a prescribed tension is the first real stumbling block for many beginners, and even for experienced knitters. Some work out a satisfactory tension for a particular stitch and garment pattern and for a particular make and count of yarn, and simplify the problem in this way. Though useful for mass production, this method is hardly a recipe for creative work.

Why tensions vary

Getting the same tension as another knitter isn't easy, even if you follow the instructions exactly and use the prescribed yarn and stitch pattern, make of machine or size of knitting needle, and even if your knitting does conform to the 'average' tension. There are several reasons why it isn't always easy to duplicate a given tension. First of all, knitting tension, whether you knit by hand or machine, is as individual as handwriting; no two people will produce *exactly* the same tension. The differences may be very slight, and therefore negligible. Where the differences are greater, one is generally advised to change to a higher or lower needle size, or to change the tension number on the dial of one's machine so that one can more nearly reproduce a

specified tension. Unfortunately this still doesn't always solve the problem; even if you get the number of stitches right, the rows may still not coincide. And, apart from the individual knitter's tension, yarn varies too; it varies not only with the specific yarn thickness or type but even with the colour of the same type of yarn, as pointed out in Chapter 5. Not only that: one knitting machine differs, however slightly, from another, even of the same model.

All this strongly suggests that a very different approach would be helpful. Most people don't find it difficult to learn to hand or machine knit; it's only a question of learning the knit stitch, the purl stitch, or how to thread-up and slide the carriage along the needlebed of a knitting machine, how to do some basic shaping and how to make a few stitch patterns. Everything goes along splendidly, and the new knitter is ready to make the first garment.

How to knit a garment without a pattern

It's in trying to follow the very first garment pattern that people sometimes become dispirited, and even give up knitting altogether. Using your own fabric as a basis for your garment should help to prevent this. Rather than choosing a pattern, buying the recommended yarn, and using the needle size or machine tension it's written for, I'd like you to consider using yarn you may already have or would like to use and any needles or knitting machine you own or can get hold of. I'd like you to be able to make a garment with these, without referring to a specific pattern; the pattern I shall refer to is merely an example, and is written up for any knitting method as a reference and to suggest pattern variations.

Simple shapes–rectangles I'm going to start with the simplest possible shape for knitting a garment, either by hand or machine: a rectangle. With at most two sizes of rectangle it's easy to make what I think of as the most basic sweater. (See

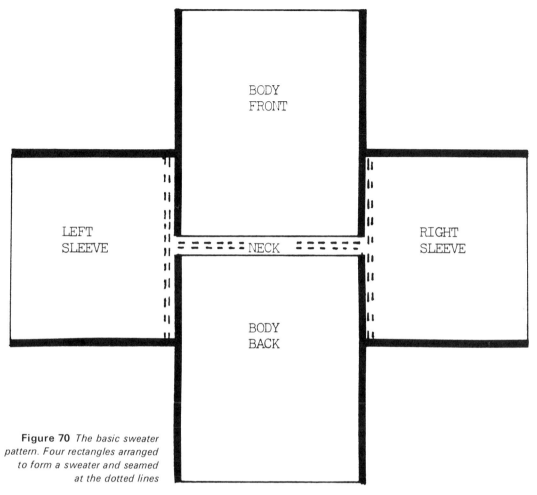

BODY
FRONT

LEFT
SLEEVE

NECK

RIGHT
SLEEVE

BODY
BACK

Figure 70 *The basic sweater pattern. Four rectangles arranged to form a sweater and seamed at the dotted lines*

figures 70 and 71.) I've made many garments based on this idea, for my family and myself, and I've found it very versatile indeed. You won't get a sophisticated garment, but you will get a useful and hard-wearing one, and – knitted to the right size, in the right yarn and given the right finish – it could even be glamorous. Above all, the simple pieces allow you to be quite creative, and, with no difficult shaping to grapple with, there's little chance of frustration. The pattern is simply this: two equal rectangles of the right size for the sleeves, and two equal ones for the front and back. I'm adding the pattern for a matching scarf which can do duty as a tension swatch. The 10 cm (4 in.) square usually suggested for a tension swatch is really not large enough for a beginner; knitting a scarf will give practice in plain or pattern knitting, and make for greater accuracy in measuring. It will also produce a viable garment.

Decide your own size and measurements You decide on the dimensions of the rectangles for yourself; you'll see from plate 1 (facing p. 72) that the result will be a drop-shoulder sweater with a slit neckline. Apart from being easy to knit, a garment made along these lines, in a suitable fabric, can be worn back to front, and possibly inside out, and this will give it more even, and so longer, wear.

It's a good idea to look through your wardrobe for similar casual sweaters and then decide what you like best about each one. Perhaps one is just the right body length, another the right width, yet another has the right sleeve length. Make a note of these measurements. People's tastes vary, of course, as they do in the amount of 'ease' they prefer. Ease is the extra width allowed in a garment to make it comfortable to wear. As knitwear is flexible, it often needs much less ease than woven fabric. Some people like their knitwear 'skin tight' and even make

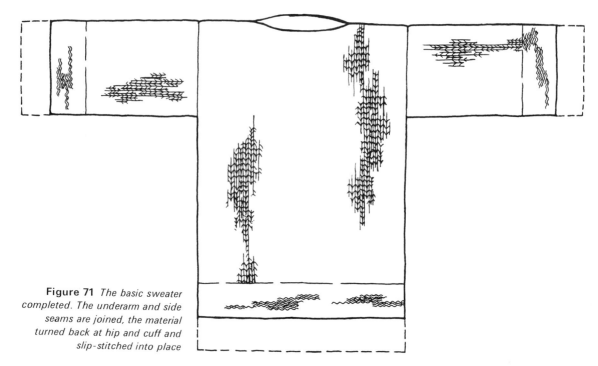

Figure 71 *The basic sweater completed. The underarm and side seams are joined, the material turned back at hip and cuff and slip-stitched into place*

it *smaller* than the actual body measurements; in effect, their bodies shape the simple, flexible structure. Others like it baggy and make it *larger*. For garments which are to be worn over other garments, like jackets, you need to consider how much more width to allow. If you take the trouble to work out just what you like, and why, you'll find it easier to make your garments as you wish them to be.

I'm going to use a medium (2/10s) Shetland wool combined with a doubled 2-ply mohair-mixture yarn in two colours to produce a fairisle sweater with a dropped-sleeve length of 49 cm (19¼ in.), a sleeve width of 40 cm (15¾ in.), a shoulder to hem length of 62 cm (24½ in.), and a half chest measurement of 45 cm (17¾ in.). The size of the rectangles to be knitted will be 40 cm × 49 cm (15¾ in. × 19¼ in.) for the sleeves, and 45 cm × 62 cm (17¾ in. × 24½ in.) for the body pieces. A useful size for a scarf would be roughly 150 cm (59 in.) long and 50 cm (19¾ in.) wide, to be doubled up to 25 cm (9¾ in.) or left as it is. These are all easy to make by any knitting method. (See figure 72.) You, of course, may prefer quite different yarns, stitch patterns or dimensions.

Choosing your own yarn and tools I'm going to suggest that you take whatever yarn you wish to knit with and combine it with whatever stitch pattern you like. Not completely without thought, of

course; a good knitted fabric is produced by using the right yarn with the right needle size or tension dial number to make a loop of the correct size. The chart opposite should be a useful guide on where to start; but there's no law to prevent you from suiting yourself about the choice of combinations. You may not have the needle size usually recommended for the thickness of yarn you're using, and trying an unusual size may give unexpectedly good results. It may also be disastrous, but, unless you try, you'll never find out! Fancy yarns, in particular, often give excellent results used at unusual tensions for their thickness, and only experiment will lead to interesting inventions. The fabrics for the chart were knitted in stocking stitch in a smooth wool yarn. Other stitch patterns, fairisle, oiled wool and fancy yarns will often need different, usually larger, needle sizes or dial numbers to produce a successful fabric.

The yarn thicknesses used in the chart are given in the terms used by most suppliers; there's a column for some worsted counts equivalents so that you have some basis for comparison. As I stressed in Chapter 5, the usual 'ply' terms are rather vague, and one supplier's 3-ply may be roughly equivalent to another's 4-ply. The amount of twist varies from soft to hard in each category.

I'd like to stress that this chart is just a guide; you shouldn't feel bound by it, it's simply there as a short cut to help you find a combination of yarn and

Tension chart
Standard tensions

Yarn			Needle size			Tension dial number*	Tension assembly number	Rows/ 10 cm (4 in.)	Stitches/ 10 cm (4 in.)
	Count	*Ply*	*UK*	*mm*	*US*				
Single	2/16s	Very fine	13	2·25	0	2	4–5	48	36
Double	2/32s	1–2-ply	12	2·5	1	3		44	34
			11	3	2	4		40	32
Double	2/24s	Fine	11	3	2	4	3–4	40	32
	2/28s	3-ply	10	3·25	3	5		38	30
Treble	2/32s		9	3·5	4	6		36	28
Single	2/8s	Medium	10	3·25	3	6	2–3	36	28
Double	2/16s	4-ply	9	3·5	4	7		34	26
			8	4	5	8		32	24
Single	3/8s	Thick	10	3·25	3	8	2	36	26
	6/17s	Double Knitting	8	4	5	9		32	24
			6	5	7	10		28	22
		Very thick	8	4	5	8 *Alternate*	1	30	22
		Triple knitting	6	5	7	9 *needles*		26	20
			4	6	9	10		22	18
		Bulky	6	5	7	8 *Third*	1	24	18
		Mohair	4	6	9	10 *needle*		22	16

* For 4·5mm pitch machines

needle or dial number which will give good results, and to avoid your wasting time trying to knit, say, treble knitting yarn with a 2·5 mm (US size 0) needle.

Choosing your fabric tension Consider now whether you like your knitted fabric to be very stiff, fairly stiff, fairly loose or very loose. You can easily decide what you like best by handling various knitted garments you have among your own or your family's clothes; some knitted fabrics are very tightly worked, some quite loosely – you'll soon feel which is which. If you like loose fabric, choose a large needle or high tension number for the type of yarn; if you like tight fabric, choose a small needle or a low tension number.

You can now use the chart to give you a second piece of vital information: roughly how many stitches to cast on for a particular width. The chart gives the average number of stitches and rows in a 10 cm

(4 in.) square, the smallest practical size for avoiding gross errors of calculation. As I've said, it's for stocking stitch fabric knitted in a smooth wool yarn. Don't expect to get precisely the same numbers; if it was as easy as that, we wouldn't have to work so hard! What the chart does is to give you the basis for an *estimate* of the number of stitches to cast on for a particular width. I know of no magic formula which will enable you to discard the tension swatch entirely, but I think you'll find that what follows will help you to cut down substantially on the time it takes to produce the right size of knitwear.

How to knit a tension swatch I use the scarf to mark out a tension swatch; if you don't want to knit the scarf, knit at least 60 stitches by 80 rows and mark out the 40 stitch, 60 row rectangle in the way suggested below for the scarf. Always mark out the centre of the swatch: cast on, cast off or edge stitches could distort the measurement. Don't

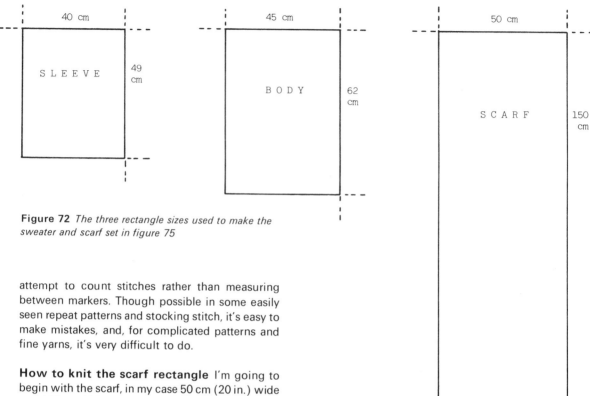

Figure 72 *The three rectangle sizes used to make the sweater and scarf set in figure 75*

attempt to count stitches rather than measuring between markers. Though possible in some easily seen repeat patterns and stocking stitch, it's easy to make mistakes, and, for complicated patterns and fine yarns, it's very difficult to do.

How to knit the scarf rectangle I'm going to begin with the scarf, in my case 50 cm (20 in.) wide and 150 cm (60 in.) long, rounding up the imperial equivalents to reasonable numbers. The medium Shetland wool and doubled mohair mixture yarns I've chosen knit up well in the traditional fairisle patterns I've adapted. These can be hand knitted, or worked – by hand or automatically – on any knitting machine. Read the chart in figure 73 by purling odd rows from right to left, and knitting even rows from left to right.

The chart suggests the use of a size 3.25 mm (US size 3) needle, or a tension dial setting of 6, for knitting a soft twist, medium weight yarn. Knitting fairisle using a doubled yarn will need a much looser tension than stocking stitch. I'm going to use my machine set at 8 because this setting has given me good results in the past.

Estimating the number of stitches Using the soft twist, medium weight line on the chart to estimate the number of stitches to cast on, my calculations will be: the width in cm (in.) times the number of stitches in 10 cm (4 in.), then dividing the result by 10 (4) – that is $(50 \times 28) \div 10 = 140$ for the metric calculation, or $(20 \times 28) \div 4 = 140$ for the imperial one. At this stage some people worry that lack of arithmetical skills will let them down. No need to worry: you can buy a simple calculator; the simpler it is, the easier it will be to use for such calculations.

Placing the pattern I'm using a fairisle pattern with a largest repeat of 12 stitches, and I'd prefer to have this placed symmetrically over my scarf width. The nearest number to 140 divisible by 12 is 144. By adding 1, and casting on 145 stitches for the scarf, this particular 12 stitch repeat pattern can be symmetrically placed over the scarf width. This can be done either by repeating the 12 stitch pattern 12 times, finishing and starting the rows as given in figure 73, or alternatively by using the punchcard, figure 115, from Pattern 1. If yours is a different pattern repeat, or if it's not symmetrical or has a different symmetry, simply adjust the stitch number to what is most convenient for your pattern. These adjustments won't make much odds to the scarf width for a reasonably small pattern repeat, but they will make it look right.

Cast on, using a closed edge for machine work, and start knitting. Knit for about 20 rows on the machine, and 10 by hand. By now you should be able to judge the feel of the fabric. If not, knit on for a few rows. When you've knitted enough to make a judgment on, make it. Base your judgment on how

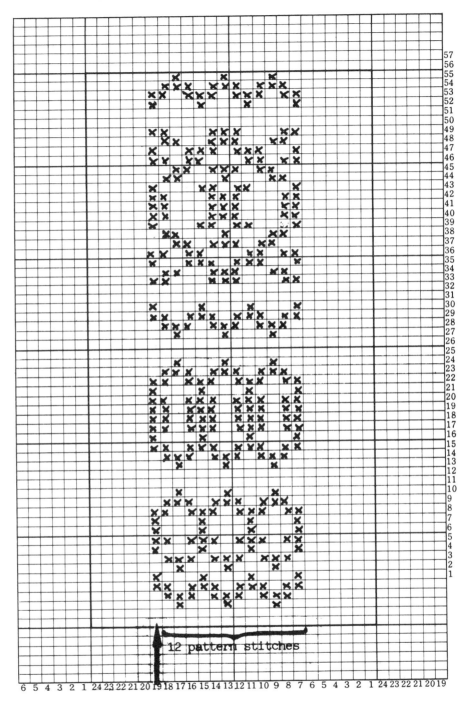

First stitch on knit rows
Last stitch on purl rows

Figure 73 *Chart for the fairisle patterns used for the sweater and scarf set in figure 75*

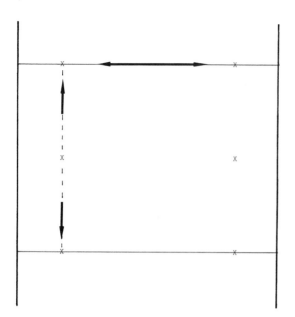

Figure 74 *How to mark a tension swatch: the Xs denote the marked stitches, the thin lines the marked rows*

pleasant you find the knitting, as well as on the feel of the fabric. Is the knitting easy to do? Does the carriage slide across the needlebed without much difficulty? Are you enjoying the knitting? Do you like the pattern? If the answer to all these questions is yes, carry on, making a note of the needle size or dial number for future reference. If not, start again with a different tension, yarn or stitch pattern.

Estimating the number of rows Once your satisfied, you can get a rough idea of how many rows to knit by using the chart gain. In this case the 150 cm (60 in.) length will need to be multiplied by 36 and divided by 10 (4), that is the calculation will be $(150 \times 36) \div 10 = 540$ rows using metric measurements, and $(60 \times 36) \div 4 = 540$ rows using imperial ones. There are 60 rows for each complete pattern in the design I'm using, and I shall knit 536 rows, that is 9 complete pattern repeats minus 4 rows so that the scarf starts and ends in a similar way. This should give me roughly the length I'd like. But first I must mark out the tension swatch.

How to mark a tension swatch Take two pieces of contrasting yarn and put them over the 21st needle on the left of 0 and the 21st needle on the right of 0, or thread them through the first and last of 42 central stitches on your needle. Take a piece of contrasting coloured cotton and knit it into the next row. Now knit 30 rows. Mark the same stitches as before with contrasting yarn. Continue knitting for a further 30 rows, then knit in another piece of

contrasting cotton with the next row, again marking the same stitches. Figure 74 shows the marked area.

The fairisle pattern I'm using could be measured without markers by simply using the known and easily seen pattern repeats; but marking the 40 stitch, 60 row rectangle is quick to do and much safer.

Go on knitting the scarf to 536 rows, then cast off *loosely*, as explained in Chapter 3. All the markers can be readily pulled out after the scarf is finished and the marked area has been measured.

The tension swatch is knitted and, with any luck, a scarf as well. Am I assuming a lot of luck? I don't think so; the measurements for a scarf are, after all, fairly arbitrary. The length is a matter of personal taste and is in any case simple to adjust: too long – it's easy to undo some of the knitting; too short – it's easy to add a piece, or to have a long fringe at both ends; too wide – it can be turned into a shawl. I don't suppose it will be too narrow, but if it is, give it to a child. As it turns out, my scarf measures 54 cm ($21\frac{1}{4}$ in.) wide and 185 cm ($72\frac{3}{4}$ in.) long without fringes. This shows very clearly that my actual tension is quite different from the estimate I got from the chart. All the same, I've got a perfectly acceptable scarf – rather a nice one, actually. (See figure 75.) All in all, I think you can get away with having knitted a scarf, and you'll have a marked tension swatch at the same time. No less important, you'll have gained practice in knitting reasonably long rows in a particular yarn and stitch pattern, and you'll be able to judge the look of the pattern properly by seeing it on a large piece. A small tension swatch can be quite deceptive; the patterns and colours may well look different in a larger piece.

Preparing the swatch for measuring Before we go on to the garment, the swatch will need washing or steaming for really accurate results. Don't be alarmed, it's not actually going to make more work for you, it's going to mean you have a beautifully smooth garment which doesn't need pressing. Finish the scarf as you wish, referring to Pattern 1 for suggestions. Now follow the washing instructions in Chapter 8, being careful to keep the markers in place. When a piece of fabric is knitted, whether by hand or machine, and with whatever type of fibre, there will always be a certain tension in the piece. This tends to be greater with machine than hand knitting, but even hand knitting will have some tension in it, partly because the yarn itself will still be tensioned (it was tensioned in the process of spinning and possibly in the process of winding it into a ball or cone), partly because the knitting will add some twist and consequently some tension. If you now take the piece and thoroughly wet it, the yarn will untension itself and take on the shape that it will always have, unless once again you put it under tension – by pressing, for example. If you don't press it, you'll always get the shape you originally knitted, except for any fibre shrinkage which may occur because the yarn itself was unstabilised or untreated. So, for a really accurate measurement of your tension swatch, wash and dry the piece and then measure it.

The rectangle, marked out by 40 stitches and 60 rows, is chosen because Knitmaster supply a very useful aid they call the 'green ruler', available from most knitting machine suppliers. One side of the ruler has numbers marked on it which relate to rows, the other numbers which relate to stitches. By laying the ruler against your marked rectangle, you can read off the number of stitches and rows which your tension produces in a 10 cm (4 in.) square. In other words, it saves you the trouble of calculating.

How to measure a tension swatch It's very important to measure correctly between the marked stitches and rows. This sounds simple, but there can be hidden pitfalls for beginners. For fabric knitted in stocking stitch or other flat fabrics, it's only necessary to lay the swatch on an even, horizontal surface, and smooth it into shape without in any way forcing it – though the method suggested below for ribbed or patterned fabric is more accurate. Measure the distance between the marked stitches horizontally and between the marked rows vertically, using the 'green', or any metric or imperial ruler. (See figure 74.) For patterns involving ribbing, or any other stitches which produce particularly elastic fabric liable to 'close up', it's necessary to decide how much stretch one wishes the fabric to have; all ribbed fabrics have considerable horizontal stretch, and measuring them when they're closed up can give quite false readings for both length and breadth. I find that by putting a piece of double-sided tape on a sufficiently large piece of cardboard and pressing one row with the cotton contrast knitted into it along the tape, I can adjust the fabric width to the tension I want to use. Allow the fabric to find its proper length for the width you have chosen. Now place a further piece of double-sided tape under the second row which the contrasting cotton was knitted into.

Your length will now be properly adjusted, but your width won't be. To finish up with a rectangle,

Figure 75 *The sweater and scarf set knitted in the fairisle pattern given in figure 73*

put some more double-sided tape vertically between the two tapes holding the marked rows. Press your fabric onto these so that the marked stitches are held on the new tapes. The measurement of the distances, between the marked rows and stitches, should now be quite accurate.

Calculating the tension Using the marked rectangle on my scarf as an example, I get the following measurements:
40 stitches measures 15 cm (6 in.)
60 rows measures 21 cm ($8\frac{1}{4}$ in.)

Calculating the number of stitches The number of stitches in 10 cm (4 in.) will be given by $(40 \times 10) \div 15 = 26 \cdot 7$ using metric measurements, or $(40 \times 4) \div 6 = 26 \cdot 7$ using imperial ones; that is 27 stitches in 10 cm (4 in.), rounded off to the nearest whole number.

Calculating the number of rows The number of rows in 10 cm (4 in.) will be given by $(60 \times 10) \div 21 = 28 \cdot 6$ using metric measurements, or $(60 \times 4) \div 8\frac{1}{4} = 29 \cdot 1$ using imperial ones; that is 29 rows in 10 cm (4 in.) rounded off to the nearest whole number.

Clearly, there's scope for error, but for most work these figures are quite adequate.

When making fabric knitted on a double bed machine, you have to remember to count the stitches on *both* beds. When knitting with left-out needles on either or both beds, you must remember to take that into account.

Working out the pattern Using the tension of 27 stitches and 29 rows to 10 cm (4 in.), the number of *stitches* to cast on for any given width will be given by: (width in centimetres $\times 27) \div 10$ for metric measurements, and (width in inches $\times 27) \div 4$ for imperial ones. The number of *rows* to knit will be given by: (length in centimetres $\times 29) \div 10$ for metric measurements, and (length in inches $\times 29) \div 4$ for imperial ones. The results of these calculations for my particular measurements tell me to cast on 108 (106) stitches for my sleeves, and to knit for 142 (140) rows; and to cast on 122 (120) stitches for the back and front, and to knit for 180 (178) rows. Before going ahead it's worth thinking for a moment. I've said you can make a perfectly good garment with just four rectangles, and this is quite true. I could go ahead and knit the four pieces, then sew them up, finishing off by double crocheting round those edges which would otherwise roll back on themselves. But, depending on the pattern, it might be as well to consider how it would fit onto the piece we're going to knit. A difference of a few stitches or rows will not appreciably alter the size of the piece, but it could appreciably alter the look of the garment.

Consider the sleeve. My pattern is a fairisle whose largest pattern repeat is 12 stitches and whose row repeat is 60. I need to cast on 108 (106) stitches; adding 1 (3) stitches will give me symmetry for the largest pattern. The length is to be 142 (140) rows: this is two complete patterns plus 22 (20) rows. I could make a plain cuff in mock or true rib equivalent to,

say, 20 rows in length, and then knit the 120 pattern rows plus 2 in stocking stitch to end with 2 plain rows. There are a number of other alternatives, but this is the quickest, easiest and most conventional.

The body pieces present no real problems; 121 stitches will make the pattern symmetrical and 180 rows give precisely three pattern repeats.

I might also give some thought to the type of finished edges or welts I'd like on my garment before starting to knit. You will see how I chose to solve this problem for the pattern written up in Chapter 9; what I'm trying to stress here is that you have several choices, and might well improve the look of the garment, and save yourself work later on, by careful judgment now.

Working the sleeves before the body gives an extra check on the tension: sleeves, like scarves, have a certain leeway in their make-up. A little too long, and it's easy enough to take off a piece, or, simpler still, to turn back the cuff; too short – use them as three-quarter sleeves; too wide – gather at the wrist to form a puffed sleeve shape; too narrow – pass the garment to a child! In fact, once you have some experience, it's even possible to use the sleeve as the tension swatch in the first place, so long as you mark out a sufficiently large rectangle well away from any side shaping, steam that portion, and allow it to dry before measuring it. For finishing methods and pattern variations see Chapter 9, Pattern 1.

Summary of the method So, to get our garment pieces, we had to:

(1) Choose a yarn and stitch pattern and decide on the dimensions of the sleeve and body rectangles.

(2) Use the tension chart to get the approximate needle size or dial number for the chosen yarn, then use it again to estimate the number of stitches to cast on and the number of rows to knit, taking account of the pattern.

(3) Cast on and knit for 10 or 20 rows, assess the work on the basis of its feel, its looks and the ease and pleasure of the knitting, and, if not satisfied, start again at a different tension, or in a different yarn, or with a different stitch pattern. Once satisfied, continue knitting and mark out a 40 stitch, 60 row rectangle for measuring later.

(4) Knit the estimated number of rows.

(5) Finish the piece, then wash or steam it, and allow it to dry.

(6) Measure the marked rectangle very carefully.

(7) Use the measurements to work out the number of stitches and rows in a 10 cm (4 in.) square, or read this off using the 'green' ruler. *This gives the tension*, and forms the basis for the calculations to give the number of stitches and rows needed for each garment piece.

(8) Consider the pattern placing and the welts before knitting the pieces.

That's all there is to it: you have your own personal pattern, and there's no need to spend time producing tension swatches which are not easily made to coincide with the one in a particular pattern. You're at liberty to change the yarn and the stitch pattern without running any risk of getting the sizing wrong. You do need to do a little arithmetic, but the calculator will do the actual figuring for you.

As I've said, I'm quite clear that this method has a great many advantages, but if you prefer to use my tension, and the yarn and measurements I've used, you're quite free to do so. You'll avoid the arithmetic, but not the tension swatch, and you'll end up with my idea of fit for a particular body size, my choice of yarn and my choice of stitch pattern. Of course, you may prefer to use and 'follow' other patterns too.

The rectangular shape isn't only the easiest to knit, by hand or machine, it's also used for a great many pattern pieces. Apart from the pieces for the basic sweater we've just made, many other garment pieces – as well as cushion covers, place mats, curtains, wall-hangings, floor coverings, and so on – are rectangular in shape. The method has you designing your own knitting patterns without even realising it.

Cut and sew

Machine knitters can make fabric by the metre (yard) very quickly. The width will depend on the machine, the yarn or combination of yarns, and the tension chosen, but the length is up to the knitter. This fabric can be used for 'cut and sew', that is dressmaking, in much the same way as bought fabric. A few suggestions on how to prepare this fabric for sewing are made in Chapter 8. One disadvantage of cut-and-sew is that the method is wasteful of yarn; another, that the thicker and more textured yarns and patterns will produce fabric which needs expert dressmaking techniques for successful making up.

Yarn wastage can be reduced by making a separate rectangle for each garment piece, just wide and long enough to accommodate the pattern.

Knitted fabric is directional, and, though this doesn't always affect the look of the two directions, it's best to knit a separate rectangle for each garment piece and to consider how to place the stitch pattern. It's not necessary, of course, to cast on and off for pieces of the same width; these can simply be separated by starting the piece in one contrasting yarn colour and finishing it in another. For long pieces, it's useful to mark every 20 or 30 rows with contrasting yarn laid over the edge needles; this helps with cutting out. Parts of the neck and other shapings can also be marked out with contrasting yarns.

A popular compromise between cut and sew and shaped knitting is to do the simple shaping as you knit and to use cut and sew methods for necklines or other complicated shapes.

Designing shaped pieces

One of the advantages of knitting your own fabric is that you can shape pattern pieces as you knit, and so avoid all cutting out. Once you've realised the advantages of working with your own fabric and tension, you may well wish to design your own shaped pieces.

Charting devices

If you have a charting device, there's no problem. The devices are supplied with a number of pattern shapes, and these are quite adequate for beginners. After you've understood the principles, you can draw your own shapes and feed them into the device, or adapt paper dressmaking patterns.

Designing your own shapes

Knitters who don't own a charting device can easily learn how to make simple shapes for themselves. As knitted fabric is so flexible, it's not often necessary to have very complicated shapes for a garment, but again, once you've understood the principles, you'll be able to work out any shape you want.

Designing knitwear is outside the scope of this book, but three common types of shaping are very briefly explained below. Difficult neck shapings in complicated stitch patterns are best left until you've had some experience; by then you'll have decided which are the best methods for you.

Tapered side shaping Shaping the side edges of the fabric symmetrically while knitting isn't difficult and it's done for many different garment pieces: skirt panels, sleeves below the armhole, V-necks, raglan sleeve heads, shoulder shaping, waist shaping, and so on. What is wanted is to taper evenly: from narrow to wide by increasing a number of stitches in a number of rows, or from wide to narrow by decreasing them. There are two types: steep shaping, where a relatively small number of stitches is to be increased or decreased in a large number of rows – for a skirt panel knitted from waist to hem, for example; or shallow shaping, where a relatively large number of stitches is to be decreased or increased in a small number of rows – to shape the shoulders in a garment knitted from waist to neck, for example. The line drawings below are not drawn to scale, and the numbers used are simply to illustrate the principles; they are not intended as patterns. You will notice that a shaped edge will be slightly longer than the original length it was based on. So one has to consider, for a particular pattern piece knitted at a particular tension, how many rows are needed to give the best length for the particular purpose. The underarm seam of a long sleeve, for instance, might be uncomfortably long if the number of rows isn't adjusted. Naturally, for a very long, flared skirt panel, this difference could be even more pronounced. On the other hand, this difference in length is often ignored, and, though this doesn't matter for shorter pieces, it very evidently affects skirts and dresses.

Steep shaping *Increasing 30 stitches to 42 stitches in 154 rows*. To achieve the tapered shaping from narrow to wide we would need to increase 12 stitches symmetrically and evenly; that is, we would need to increase $12 \div 2 = 6$ times, 1 stitch at both ends of a particular row, at regular intervals. There will be $6 + 1 = 7$ intervals, as shown in figure 76.

The slanting edge will be longer than the centre of the piece, and I'm assuming we wish to take account of this by reducing the number of rows to be knitted. How many depends on the particular circumstances, but assume that the 154 rows are to be reduced to 142, that is by 12 rows, to allow for this. We want our 7 intervals to be spread among the 142 rows as evenly as possible, so our calculation will be $142 \div 7 = 20$ and 2 over. Our intervals will be 20 rows each with 22 in one. This is placed where it fits in best with the particular pattern piece.

If the number of intervals is much greater, say 25 over 142 rows, a more even shape is produced by a set of, say, 6-row intervals followed by a set of 5-row intervals, or some other convenient combination.

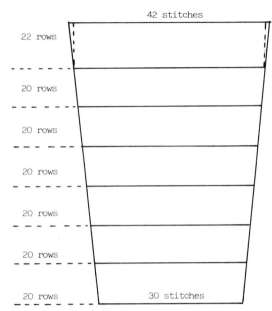

42 stitches

22 rows

20 rows

20 rows

20 rows

20 rows

20 rows

20 rows

30 stitches

Figure 76 *Steep side shaping. The shaped piece will have reasonably smooth sides – the flexibility of the knitting compensating for the slight geometric inaccuracy*

Shallow shaping *Reducing 126 stitches to 40 stitches in 8 rows*. The number of stitches to be decreased will be $126 - 40 = 86$. For symmetrical decreasing we would wish to divide this as evenly as possible among the 8 rows: $86 \div 8 = 10$ and 6 over. The usual method is to cast off 11 stitches at the beginning of the first 6 rows, then 10 at the beginning of the next 2 rows. If, instead, you use held stitches at the ends of the rows, you'll be able to cast off over all the held stitches in one operation and you'll end up with two smooth lines rather than a series of steps. (See figure 77.)

It's possible to make quite reasonable approximations to curves by casting off, or holding, a number of stitches at the beginning or end of several rows. Concave, convex and mixed curves can all be produced in this way.

Convex curve In order to make the centre length equal to the side length of a symmetrically tapered piece, we can use held stitches to add a curve. This is particularly important for skirt or dress panels, otherwise the seams are longer than the central sections and an unattractive dip appears at the seams. It's also often helpful for wide, rectangular sleeves. (See figure 121.) Figure 78 shows one way of producing a convex curve in 12 rows.

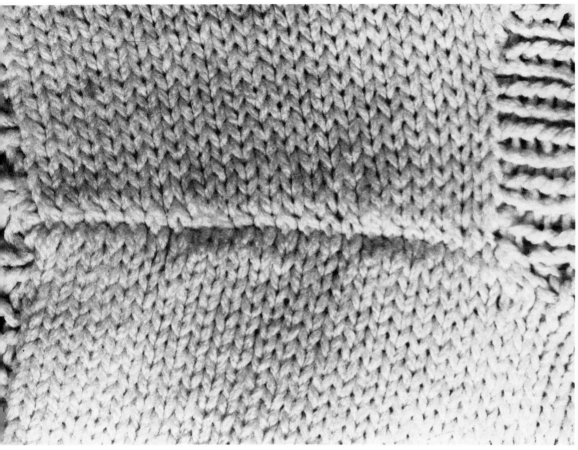

Figure 77 *A neat shoulder seam. The holding position was used to shape the shoulder on the back and front body sections of the garment. The two pieces were cast off together*

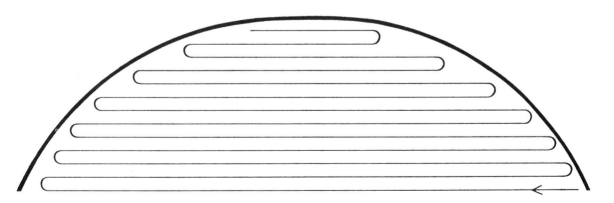

Figure 78 *Making a convex curve: this curve was shaped by putting stitches into the holding position at the ends of each of 12 rows, then casting off over all the stitches*

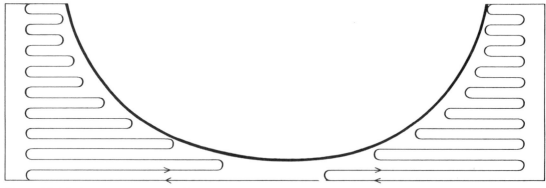

Figure 79 *Making a concave curve: this curve was made in two parts, first by knitting the right hand side, then by knitting the left hand side*

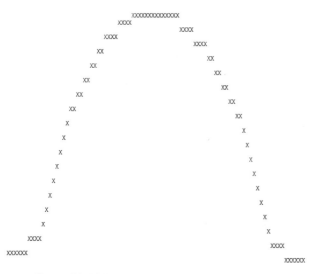

Figure 80 *Making a shaped sleeve head: casting off – or putting in holding – the stitches represented by the Xs in the diagram, will result in a curve very similar to the ones used for sleeve heads in dressmaking patterns*

Concave curve To hollow out a garment piece, for a neckline, for instance, we can again use held stitches, but this time the shaping is from the centre of the garment piece rather than from the edge. When knitting by hand, or with a machine which allows you to feed the yarn by hand, it's possible to shape both sides at the same time by using two separate yarn balls. For other machines, it's usual to keep one side in holding, or to knit the stitches back to the non-working position, while working the other side. The second side is worked when the first side has been finished. Figure 79 shows a concave curve made in two parts. (See figure 64).

Mixed curves An ordinary sleeve head worked from armhole to shoulder consists of shallow shaping at the armholes, more rapid shaping between the armhole and the sleeve head, and shallower shaping at the sleeve head itself. In fact the shaping is a combination of concave, tapered side and convex shaping, and figure 80 shows how this combination produces a curve quite similar to the ones used in dressmaking patterns. You can, of course, shape this curve as you like, making either a shallow or a deep sleeve head.

The curves can be knitted at the beginning or at the end of a particular garment piece. For example, Pattern 3, in Chapter 9, starts at the neckline.

Using graph paper Though ordinary graph paper is useful for charting shapes in the initial stages, don't forget that most knitting tensions aren't equal in rows and stitches; there are usually more rows than stitches to the unit length. Ordinary graph paper won't produce the right shape, though it's possible to buy paper which is nearer to the average knitting tension. (See figure 73.)

Using mistakes

You'll find that after a while you get to know how to shape a particular pattern piece without having to make extensive calculations; you'll get to know what is needed for a particular shape and size. By using these methods you get a 'feel' for fabric, stitch and pattern design. Even if your first efforts don't work out as you'd hoped, don't be discouraged. After all, a rectangular sleeve which is too long and wide can be used as the body piece for a sweater. In fact, most knitted pieces can be used in *some* pattern piece – even if it's only a patch pocket. I once knitted a sleeve which was both too short and too narrow, in a mock Aran fabric. Folding it over sideways, I realised that I'd knitted a collar; I made it detachable.

Figure 81 *A knitted collar*

(See figure 81.) Just use your ingenuity, and, above all, feel confident that *you* can do it.

The trick is to turn disadvantages into advantages. To illustrate this, let me tell you about my favourite mistake. I was intending to use Knitmaster card 2 for a simple all-over tuck pattern. I worked out my garment pieces, started with a full needle rib for a wide hip band, then transferred the stitches from the ribber to the single bed, ready to start the tuck pattern. I changed the tension, aligned the needles, started off . . . and forgot the punchcard release lever! Three rows later I realised what had happened. Hopeful as ever about the advantages of mistakes, I looked at the piece I'd just knitted; I could see that it looked promising. What about switching to plain knitting – stockinet – for a few rows? then back to three rows of tuck? I thought; and carried on. The result was the sweater in figure 4. In fact I'd accidentally stumbled on a quick and easy way of making bobble effect fabrics in machine knitting. But that wasn't all. It took a few more weeks, but suddenly I realised that on either side of my bobble was a convenient hole; I could use the bobbles to thread elastic through: an easy way to get a casing, for elastics at waist, wrist and neck. And if I could thread elastic through, I could thread anything through – so what about using the holes to make some interesting patterns with crochet chains, or leather thongs, or machine-made cording? Another opportunity for unusual effects. Figure 82 shows one way of using this technique.

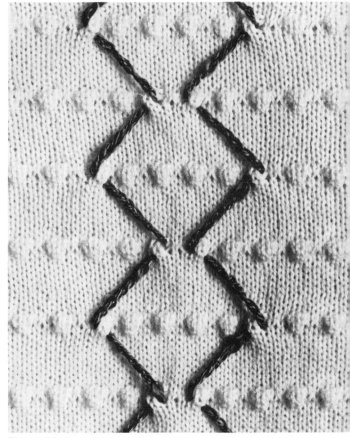

Figure 82 *Tuck stitch used to make a mock bobble stitch. The holes on both sides of the bobble can be used for threading elastic, ribbon or chain crochet*

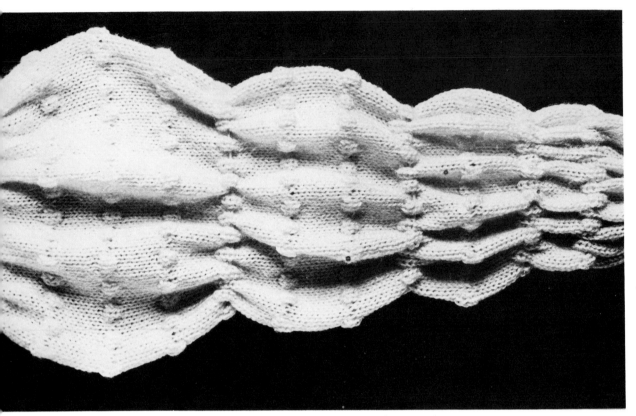

Figure 83 *Elastic threaded through some of the rows of a blouse sleeve knitted in tuck stitch*

What if I made a hem, and the three rows of tuck were at the edge? A simple and easy way to make a finish similar to picot, I thought. This would make a suitable edging for all kinds of children's clothes, collars, blouses. And if I found I didn't like it, I could just slip elastic through the bottom edge to make an easy blouson. In fact I could make a quite different fabric by slipping elastic through several rows – rather like using shirring elastic on a sewing machine. Figure 83 shows shirring used on a sleeve at different distances.

You see? Not all mistakes have happy endings, of course, but surprisingly many do. So give them a chance to work out well.

7 NEW MATERIAL

The tools are ready, the yarns chosen and the basic skills acquired; the time has come to produce the fabrics. That's what it's all about – the crafted fabric. Once you have the skills, the yarns and the tools, and the will to apply them boldly, you'll certainly be able to produce that entirely individual product – the new material.

Clearly some stitch patterns will have to be used; even the simplest hand knitting instruction to knit every stitch on every row, or machine knitting instruction to knit stockinet, involves a stitch pattern which produces a certain fabric. But stitch patterns aren't the only things that will produce a variety of fabrics. Even with very few stitch patterns a great many original fabrics can be produced by judiciously using one, or a combination, of the following simple methods.

Easy ways to produce new material

(1) The effect of the stitch pattern can be varied by using different tensions within one piece.

(2) Yarns can be chosen in unusual colour and fibre combinations, textures, texture combinations, random colourings, bead- or sequin-threaded and doubled to give a great variety of fabrics.

(3) The look of the stitch pattern can be changed by changing the direction of the knitting: up or down, sideways, on the bias, or using the 'wrong' side.

(4) More than one stitch pattern can be used within a single piece, or for different pieces of a garment or other article.

(5) The fabric can be embossed after knitting by crocheting, weaving or embroidering on its surface.

(6) Knitting and weaving can be combined.

Machine knitters can readily increase this range by:

(7) Leaving some needles in the non-working position to increase the range of usable yarns and to create laces.

(8) Using a particular punchcard in unexpected ways by knitting with only some of the needles in the working position. New punchcards can also be designed.

(9) Using hand tools and manual stitch selection.

All these methods are easy enough for a new knitter to try out on simple shapes.

Using stitch patterns

There is a host of traditional stitch patterns available to the hand knitter and these can be collected from various sources and learned, or new patterns invented. Machine manufacturers go to a lot of trouble to produce pattern books and printed patterns for punching additional punchcards. Each punchcard can make several new fabrics by using the machine on different pattern settings and in various yarns, tensions and colourings.

A few of the well-known stitch patterns are given in Chapters 2 and 3; though you don't have to be very skilled to use them, combining these with ideas of your own based on the following suggestions should make it quite easy for you to produce satisfying original fabrics right from the start of your knitting career. The suggestions are for both hand and machine knitting; though the results will be similar, they won't be identical. The idea is to use the easiest and quickest methods to get good results in either case.

Patterning by tension

If several rows are knitted first on a loose, then on a tight tension, the effect is to give a striped texture to the knitting. Quite interesting fabrics can be made simply by knitting stocking stitch and changing the tension in various ways. For example, one might knit ten rows on a tight tension followed by four rows on a loose tension, and then continue along these lines. Or one might start at the tightest tension and progress, row by row, to the loosest. This can be

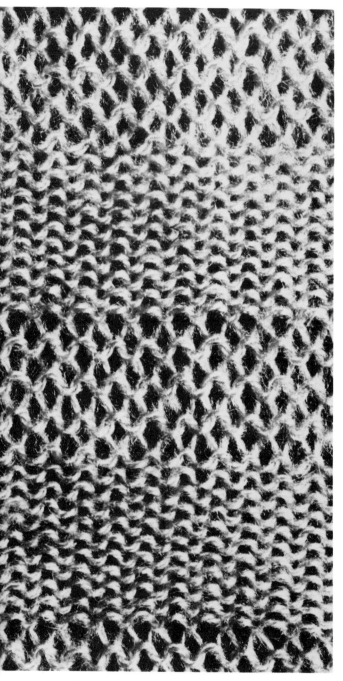

Figure 84 *Patterning by changing the tension*

done by machine or by hand, merely by changing needle sizes or tension numbers, and using any suitable stitch pattern. The first example will give the appearance of ridges, as shown in figure 84.

Shaping by tension It's possible to do some types of shaping by changing the tension; a well-known example is a hemmed neckband. Consider a 30 row band folded to make a hem. Say you start the band at a medium tension on, for example, five rows, knitting one needle size or tension point tighter for the next five rows, again decrease the tension proportionally for the next ten rows, then increase twice for the following sets of five rows; this will give a nicely shaped band for a rounded neckline, easily formed into a curve. (See figure 85.)

Another well-known method of shaping is to change the tension of a ribbed piece – a roll collar, for instance. This can be made to fit snugly round the neck and the roll-back widened simply by loosening the tension appropriately.

The tension can also be changed by varying the yarn thickness as well as, or instead of, the needle size or tension dial. A garment knitted in a medium weight yarn might be much improved by knitting the collar and cuffs with the yarn doubled. I often use this method when finishing collars by hand; I simply use two ends for part or the whole of a collar. (See figure 86.) This not only makes the fabric wider, it also makes it heavier. The extra weight can be useful for collars and cuffs and gives a better 'hang' for skirts and the lower sections of jackets, as in Pattern 3, Chapter 9.

Patterning by change of stitches

Changing the look and function of a fabric by varying the stitch pattern within the fabric piece is a well-known device. The edges of many garment pieces – cuffs, waistbands, button bands – are often knitted in a different stitch pattern from the main garment pattern. Chapter 8 gives details. The method can, however, be usefully extended by knitting the whole of a garment section in several different stitches. That is, knitting gives you the option of using different fabrics in the same garment piece, without a joining seam. The effects of the differences in tension need to be carefully noted, then used to advantage.

Aran style knitting Using different stitch patterns, not only in sets of rows but even in blocks of stitches within a row, is a traditional way for hand knitters to introduce interesting panels or sections into knitted fabric. A well-known example is Aran knitting, where different combinations of stitches giving textured fabrics are invented by the knitters; the initiated can even tell which knitter in the

community made a particular garment. Machine knitting isn't as versatile as hand knitting in this respect, unless much of the needle selection is done manually. Some double bed machines can work a number of different stitch patterns in one row, and the methods for making single motifs can be used to insert pattern sections between stockinet on many modern punchcard machines. However, the bulk of machine knitting, if it's to be done at speed, isn't well suited to this type of work.

One method of giving the illusion of Aran knitting is to knit garment pieces from side to side, using knitweave, tuck and slip stitch patterns to make strips of different fabrics. Several tensions will have to be taken into account, but interestingly textured garments can be made quite rapidly by machine.

Figure 85 *Shaping by changing the tension* (left)

Figure 86 *Shaping by knitting with different yarn thicknesses. I've left the seams undone for part of the collar to add pattern interest*

Figure 87 *Shaping by changing the stitch pattern*

Figure 87 shows a sweater knitted to the garment pattern used in Chapter 6, but with the rectangles knitted from side to side rather than up or down. All the stitch patterns used for this particular sweater are based on the tuck stitch setting, with a few rows of stockinet to show them off. The different tensions have changed the rectangular shapes so that now there are gently curved lines at the edges. The effect has been to make well-shaped sleeves, a rounded hipline and to give sufficient extra material at the neckline for a self-facing. The collar is a rectangle folded in half; the extra central width conveniently gives it shape. (See figure 81.)

There are many variations on this theme. The suggestions for using simple rectangles to make knitted garments, which follow Pattern 1 in Chapter 9, should give you many ideas for this type of knitting.

Shaping by changing stitch patterns The example just discussed shows very clearly that fabric width can be increased or decreased by a change of stitch pattern without a change of tension. Many knitweave and tuck stitch patterns will widen, and most rib stitches will narrow, a piece when compared to stocking stitch worked on the same tension. Introducing ribs at the waist of a garment is a good way to get a neat fit without much shaping. Widening – and improving the hang of – a skirt is easily and quickly done by switching to a different pattern. It's not always possible to eliminate shaping entirely, but it's certainly possible to cut down the amount one needs.

Patterning by yarns

Using two or more coloured yarns for one garment is nothing new. Even using unusual or 'fancy' yarns for some or all of the garment pieces in well-known and easily worked stitch patterns is an obvious way to produce new fabrics.

Unusual materials One of the big advantages of hand knitting is that many reasonably long and thin materials can be used to knit with. This includes ribbons and leather thongs as well as yarns, strings and even crocheted or other cords. Fabrics produced by working imaginatively with unusual materials are bound to be highly individual. Though not all yarns, let alone all the materials knittable by hand, can be used for machine knitting, a great many can be used as the weaving yarn for knitweave patterns. These need not be complicated; the simplest often anchor the yarns more securely, but the unusual material used for the weaving gives a new-look fabric. It's often possible to buy weaving yarns quite inexpensively; these tend to be too harsh for the machine knitting yarn, but can often be used as the weaving yarn and this combination can make excellent, distinctive and hardwearing clothes.

Doubling yarns I suggested in Chapter 5 that the fine, industrially coned yarns could be combined by 'doubling' them in various colour, texture and fibre mixtures. It's not, of course, necessary to confine oneself to industrially coned fine yarns;

Plate 5 *Mohair sweater knitted on every third needle on a basic machine. The brushed mohair yarn shows up well on the purl side of jersey; the collar, cuffs and hipbands were knitted by hand in single rib.*

Plate 6 *Knitwoven two-piece, the knitweave pattern used vertically in the jacket adapted from Pattern 2, and horizontally in the two-panel skirt with elasticated waist. The base yarn is an acrylic/wool mixture, the weaving yarn a tweedy bulked acrylic*

Plate 7 *Yoked jacket knitted to Pattern 2, adapted for set-in sleeves. The base yarn is a mixed-fibre double knitting worked on alternate needles, the weaving yarn a random loop yarn*

Plate 8 *Reversible tuck lace T-shirt on the left, all-over fairisle with V-neck on the right. The T-shirt was knitted in a bouclé cotton, using a punchcard machine and selected needles. The V-neck jumper was knitted in a combination of dark grey and medium blue Shetland wools*

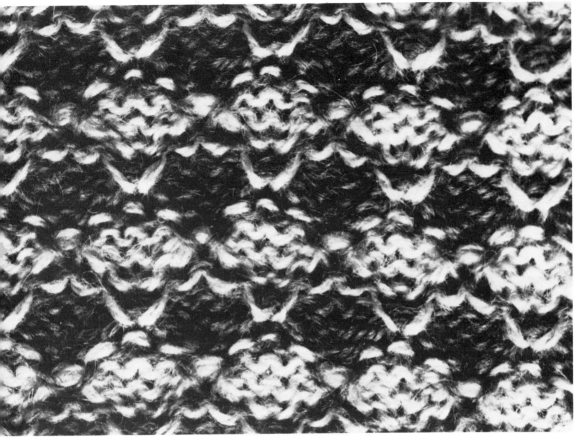

Figure 88 *The purl side of a coloured tuck stitch pattern*

adding sewing threads, and particularly glitter threads, can give a most unusual look to your own doubled yarns. For a little extra twist before knitting, it's quick to take the yarn ends you want to combine and wind them together on the yarn or cone winder; this will add just enough twist to make the knitting easier to do.

Space dyed or random yarns Random yarns have been specially manufactured to give an easy method of producing coloured patterns in a plain, usually stocking stitch, fabric; and their use can be readily extended to give even more interesting results. Most fairisle or Jacquard knitted by hand is made by using several colours for a particular garment; this isn't too arduous for the hand knitter, though it does mean keeping several yarn balls untangled, and twisting or weaving the yarns at the back to prevent holes or long floats. For punchcard machine knitting, working with more than two colours for a single garment piece is tiresome unless one has an automatic colour changer. Random yarns can give a good 'mock fairisle' effect. The method is to use one plain coloured yarn in one feeder and to choose a random yarn which will blend suitably for the second. The two yarns are used to knit the pattern, regardless of colour changes. A variation is to use two contrasting fine yarns doubled in one feeder, a plain yarn in the other. The result will be quite a good imitation fairisle, and of course it's just as quick to work as the ordinary two-colour fairisle. (See plate 1, facing p. 72.)

This is helpful even for hand knitting, as there are only two yarn balls to deal with. Weaving with random yarns when making a knitweave fabric produces unevenly striped patterns with little effort. (See plate 2, facing p. 72, and figures 102, 122.)

Coloured tuck stitch Machine knitting tuck stitch patterns in colours is a most attractive way to get textures as well as colours into the knitted fabric. Though this is somewhat tedious to do without a colour changer, as the colours are best changed for

Figure 89 *The knit side of a coloured slip stitch pattern*

every set of tucks, the results are good enough to persuade some knitters to persevere, at any rate for part of a garment. Apart from getting texture as well as colour, that bugbear of single bed fairisle knitting – the long floats – is eliminated. What's more, two sides of interesting fabric emerge, and it's well worthwhile to make a reversible garment. (See figures 88 and 42.)

Patchwork knitting Jacquard knitting, that is using more than two colours in a single row – and perhaps in stitch patterns other than stocking stitch – is much easier for the hand than for the machine knitter. However, with a little ingenuity, one can produce patchwork on a knitting machine. One obvious way is to knit in long strips of different colours, textures and stitch patterns, then to join the strips with crochet, knitting in on the machine or by the latch-up method described in Chapter 8.

For even greater variety, the holding position can be used to add coloured and textured pieces with diagonal patterning. The whole garment piece, if combined with sideways and bias knitting, can take on unusual and unexpected forms – a sort of free-style knitting, well-suited to people who enjoy spontaneity. You can use any complementary yarns in any available colours or textures. As long as the garment sections are simple, as in Pattern 1, for example, you can let your imagination go.

Coloured slip stitch Slip stitch can also be used to make multi-coloured fabrics, both by hand and machine. One advantage of this method over fairisle for the hand knitter is that only one ball of yarn is used for each row. Figure 89 shows a simple but effective 4-row pattern. A 3 knit, 1 slip stitch repeat is used for 4 rows, the colours changed and the same pattern, moved along 2 stitches or needles, is used in the second colour for the next 4 rows. These 8 rows form the pattern.

Textured slip stitch The fabrics can be made to have more texture by using a simple pattern re-

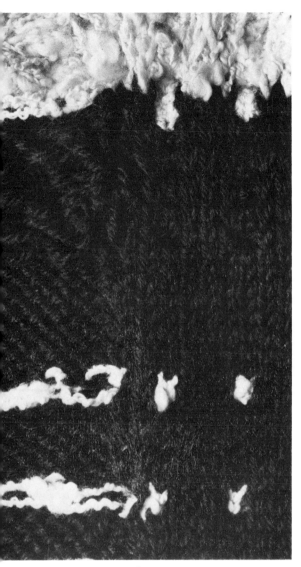

Figure 90 *From top to bottom: mock loop stitch and its reverse side, in a textured and a plain yarn; the same pattern knitted for 2 rows only between bands of jersey*

Figure 91 *Check patterns: these are easily made by interrupting vertical stripes with rows of stocking stitch*

peatedly. If only the 4th stitch, say, in every row is knitted and the other 3 slipped, and this pattern is repeated for a number of rows followed by a row of stockinet, a mock-loop fabric will be produced. Textured yarns increase the possibilities of this type of fabric (See figure 90.)

If yarns of different colours and textures are combined, even more variety can be produced. A band of reverse stocking stitch worked in a plain yarn, followed by 2 rows in the slip stitch pattern

just given and worked in a textured yarn, can give good results and is easy to do. As the textured yarn is only knitted on every 4th stitch, it's possible to use quite thick yarns, even on a knitting machine.

Checks and vertical stripes Fairisle can easily be used to produce vertical stripes; on a punchcard machine these are made by locking a card on one particular pattern row. In hand or non-automatic machine knitting they're made by repeating a particular pattern row for the whole garment piece. The reverse side is often a good two-colour mock-loop

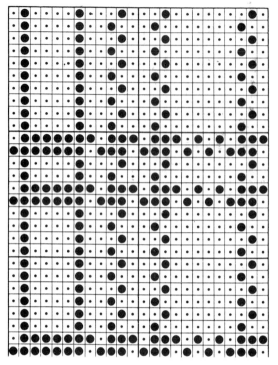

Figure 92 *Two types of check punched for a 24-space card. The right hand side check uses fairisle banding, the left hand side is similar to the pattern illustrated in figure 91*

pattern, formed by the regular floats. (See figure 21.)

To produce a number of interesting check patterns it's only necessary to interrupt the fairisle knitting with stocking stitch. Figure 91 shows one such pattern which is particularly easy to do on semi-automatic and manual machines. The checks can be made more subtle and automatic for punch-card knitting by using a fairisle banding, as shown by the punchcard in figure 92, adapted from pattern 126 in the Knitmaster Pattern Library. A check similar to the one used to knit the fabric in figure 91 is shown for purposes of comparison.

Different fibres and textures Fairisle knitting can be used to combine the yarns not only for their colour, but also for their texture, by hand or machine.

Threading the two feeders on a machine with a smooth and bouclé yarn, the same colour or toning but perhaps in different fibres, will give unexpectedly interesting fabrics. I like to use a combination of smooth wool and cotton yarns, or smooth cotton

with acrylic bouclé, or smooth wool and wool bouclé. Both sides of the fabric can be used, and the method is completely automatic on a punchcard machine. The essence of this technique is to use small, simple patterns; it's the contrasting yarn textures which make the effect. Pattern 3 uses this type of fabric as well as 'doubling' yarn.

Patterning by direction

Sideways knitting I've already referred to sideways knitting as a way of suggesting an Aran look for machine knitting. Apart from the advantages of a garment knitted in this way, some of which are clear from Pattern 2, knitting sideways gives considerable scope for extending the use of stitches already known and easily used.

To get vertical stripes without the floats inherent in fairisle knitting, horizontal bands can be turned on their side. There are a number of ways of making these bands; ridge stitches, easily made in hand knitting, make firmly textured garments in any of the bulky yarns and produce a 'different looking' garment very rapidly. The effects are improved if you vary the width of the bands, as shown in figure 121, or go from wide to narrow, for instance, or even use toning colours to merge into a shaded whole.

For hand or machine knitting, patterning by tension, using different stitch patterns, alternating different coloured yarns, or plain and textured yarns, or shiny and matt yarns, will all give interesting and quickly produced fabrics. Nothing could be simpler than to knit a matt band in a wool or cotton yarn, followed by a toning or contrasting band in shiny rayon. One of the things to bear in mind is that different types of yarn may shrink in different ways when they're washed. This isn't necessarily a disadvantage; an untreated rayon, say, combined with a non-shrink wool might produce a seersucker fabric with an interesting scalloped line at the side edges. However, the tension swatch must be carefully worked and washed, or you may get very poor results.

'Wrong' side knitting Using a knitted fabric sideways effectively doubles the number of stitch patterns; using the back or 'wrong' side of the fabric increases the number yet again. Some fabrics do, in fact, look the same on both sides; but a great many knitted fabrics are not only different but equally effective on both sides.

The purl side of stocking stitch is often used as the 'right' side; knitted in quite ordinary yarn, it makes a

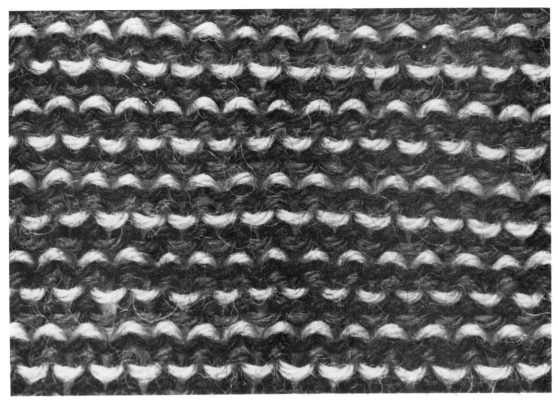

Figure 93 *The purl side of jersey knitted in single row stripes in three colours*

nice change from the usual smooth side. For some yarns the purl side isn't only a nice change, it has another advantage as well. The long pile of brushed mohair and of similar yarns is shown off to much greater effect. Using every other, or even every third, needle on a knitting machine will go some way to producing a fabric comparable to the hand knitted one. (See plate 5, facing p. 96.) The fabric can also be brushed to increase the effect.

Using the purl side of a single-row jersey stripe fabric works very well. For three colours, the knitting is quite straightforward: knit one row in each of the colours A, B and C; you are at the correct side to repeat the pattern, starting again with A. (See figure 93.) The fabric is unexpectedly tweedy, and looks well whether used vertically or horizontally.

Most of the tuck stitches so easily knitted on the machines are particularly effective on both sides; as I often can't decide which I prefer, I find it worthwhile to make them up into completely reversible garments. Some ways of making up reversible garments are mentioned in Chapter 8. (See figure 101.)

Bias knitting Yet another dimension is given to the various stitch patterns by making use of diagonal or bias knitting. This can be emphasised by knitting stripes into the bias fabric. The resulting fabric pieces, if used for a collar or cuffs, say, will give interesting slanting stripes. They can look most effective in unusual yarn combinations, or narrow glitter stripes. It's also possible to work bands of patterning instead of colours; again, the completed band will show the patterns off in an unusual way, creating the illusion of a completely new stitch. Figure 21 shows a band folded to make a collar.

Using punch lace

As I said in Chapter 3, making punch lace isn't difficult. However, it's only one method of using this pattern setting. Any machine capable of knitting true punch lace can substitute other yarns for the nylon in the second feeder; cotton thread is a well-known alternative. Using a cotton in the same colour as the yarn, or preferably a slightly darker tone of that colour, gives a lacy effect and you don't have the difficulties of using nylon. Wool and cotton combinations make good lightweight fabrics, and one is illustrated in figure 94. It's also possible to

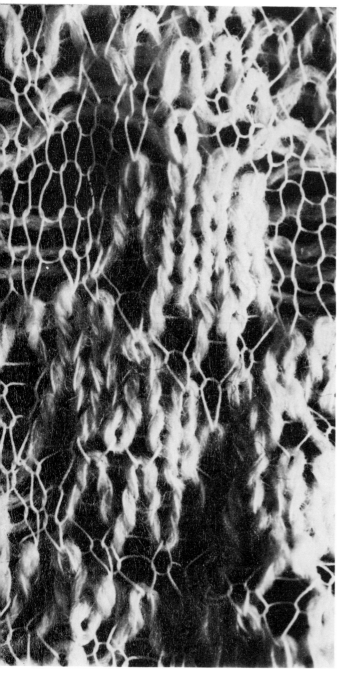

Figure 94 *Punch lace: wool combined with cotton thread*

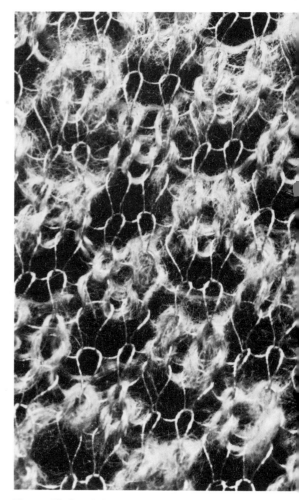

Figure 95 *Punch lace: acrylic yarn combined with glitter thread*

buy thin metallic threads. If these are used in the second feeder, a sort of chain mail fabric is produced; the metal thread lies on the knit side of the fabric, with the main yarn just behind it. With the right colour combinations, and a neat, small pattern, this can give excellent and not too garish evening fabrics. (See figure 95.)

You can also make a double-sided fabric, almost like the plate knitting on some of the Knitmasters. Take any two fine yarns, and thread them through the two feeders. Now set the machine on punch lace knitting, using a simple pattern card, and a double-sided fabric will be produced, with the occasional lace-stitch given by the single yarn. This will produce a reversible fabric which I've used for the blouson illustrated in figure 115; the sleeves are shown separately in figure 96. Fine yarns should be used so that the needles knitting both yarns together aren't overloaded. The yarn combinations should be chosen with care; I find a fine mohair mixture used with a fine random yarn particularly successful.

Figure 96 *Two sides of a punch lace fabric. The fabric has been made by using a fine mohair yarn combined with a fancy acrylic yarn*

The most suitable punchcards are those which will give the least lace, that is, a relatively small number of holes in the punchcard will give the best results.

Knitweave

Knitweave is a stitch pattern which will produce a fabric very different from the others discussed so far – a combination of knitting and weaving. It can be made by hand, by weaving a yarn into some of the stitches whilst knitting with the base yarn, or a weaving yarn can be threaded through the knitting later; but to produce a fabric reasonably quickly, a knitting machine capable of knitweave is a great asset. However, this pattern isn't completely auto-matic even on the most modern machines. The weaving yarn has to be positioned by hand on each row.

The machine threads the weaving yarn over and *through* the stitches on the side of the fabric facing the knitter. In other words, the weaving yarn doesn't actually go through to the far side of the fabric. The 'right' side is the purl side of the knitting. The pattern shows as a series of floats on the purl background, and is made by the needle selection, using a punchcard or needle selector. Actually, as knitted stitches are loops, the weaving yarn can be seen through them on the 'wrong' side, and full use can be made of this as a reversible type of fabric. (See figure 97.)

Because knitweaving is a relatively slow process, whether worked by hand or machine, it isn't used as much as it might be. In spite of the extra time involved, I like to use knitweave for a great many of my knitted garments. Time and again people have told me how lovely these fabrics are, and how much they preferred them to the results of ordinary knitting.

I think it will be helpful to go into one or two details about the use of this method and to point out a few of its advantages, to convince you that the extra work involved in making this sort of knitwear is well worthwhile. The techniques mentioned were worked out on a Knitmaster 321, but can be readily adapted to other machines.

Advantages of knitweave
Less stretch in the woven direction The knit-woven fabric isn't quite as flexible as ordinary knitted fabric. In the direction of the weave the fabric is almost as stable as ordinary softly woven fabric – that is, there is a certain 'give', but only that of the yarn itself. The actual length of the yarn across the row is very nearly the length of the row, with a little extra to account for the slight weaving in and out of the knitted stitches. So a wool yarn will have more elasticity than a cotton one. Knitweave has certain advantages for knitted skirts, dresses, trousers and jackets. Ordinary knitted fabric is so flexible that when skirts or trousers made of it are worn the material spreads as the wearer sits down. The heat of the body then helps to 'press' the material into the shape of the seat, and the result can be a somewhat unflattering bulge when the wearer stands up. The woven yarn in knitweave fabric helps to solve this problem. Because this yarn can't stretch to any great extent, the knitted backing is kept to a reasonable shape. The 'pressing' effect of weight and heat may

Figure 97 *The knit and purl side of a knitwoven fabric. The weaving yarn, though used on the purl side, shows through to the knit side*

flatten the fabric, but it doesn't make for such an unsightly bulge. Even ordinary woven fabric 'seats' up to a point, so don't expect miracles; but the resilience of knitweave makes quite a difference.

Lighter, slimmer clothes Almost any thickness of knitting yarn can be used for weaving on a knitting machine, whereas there's much more restriction for general knitting. Knitweaving has advantages over both hand and machine knitting; even though hand knitting presents no difficulties for the bulkier yarns, the fabrics produced tend to be thick, ungainly, and difficult to wash and wear. The sheer weight of yarn pulls the knitted loops out of shape. Knitweaving means you can use these yarns simply and economically, to get the benefit of their warmth and

the beauty of their looks without the disadvantage of the added bulking in a knitted loop. The fabric will be lighter, warmer, less thick. It won't add so many inches to your girth!

Cheaper clothes The bulkier yarns are not cheap to use. Knitting a row uses roughly three times as much yarn as weaving it across; a knitwoven garment will use roughly one-third of the bulky yarn needed to knit the garment; the rest of the material can be a fine to medium yarn which can often be bought economically. The result is a cheaper, as well as a more unusual, more creative fabric.

Fixed hemline If the fabric is used with the weaving in the vertical direction, so that the hemline will be along the side edges, the stretch in this direction will be quite limited. This is particularly useful for skirts, which can 'drop' considerably in ordinary knitted fabric.

Making cut and sew fabric It isn't necessary to use different weight yarns or contrasting colours for knitweaving. Very good fabrics can be made by using the same medium or fine yarn for both, and the results, particularly on a tighter tension than usual, will produce material which can be used for cut and sew without any fear of stitches running when one cuts out.

Stripes and striped effects Stripes have been discussed in some detail earlier; knitweave adds even more possibilities. It's simple to switch from ordinary knitting to knitweaving and back again; knitting for a number of rows with the backing yarn, then knitweaving for a further number of rows, creates a simply achieved striped pattern without the need for changing yarns in the feeder of a machine. The bands will be subtly related, as they're connected by the backing yarn colour. (See plates 2 and 7, facing pp. 72 and 97.)

Using several colours There's no need to keep to a single colour for the weaving yarn. It can be guided by hand rather than threaded up in the yarn brake, so it's easy to use as many colours as one wants, as long as there's a separate container to hold each one and prevent them from tangling.

Pleats A fine backing yarn combined with a fairly chunky, possibly textured weaving yarn can be used to create the illusion of pleats. Making bands of stripes, as before, creates such a difference in weight that the knitted fabric tends to sag between the knitwoven strips. Using the holding position as in Pattern 2, will give a yoke with a pleated fabric neatly attached. (See plate 2, facing p. 72.)

Lace weave The 'wrong' side of the knitweave often makes an attractive fabric without any further work. However, in order to show off the weaving yarn still more, use can be made of the lace effect one gains by putting some needles in the non-working position, or by using a transfer lace stitch for the backing fabric. A very attractive reversible fabric can be produced. (See figure 97.)

Techniques for knitweave Although knitweaving is a slow method of working, it isn't particularly difficult. However, there are a few techniques which are worth bearing in mind for machine knitting, and these could make all the difference between success and failure.

Perhaps the most important point to bear in mind is the need to have all the brushes running smoothly; in order to check that pieces of fluff aren't causing problems, take the carriage off the needlebed, turn it over, and test the brushes by twirling them. If any pieces of fluff are lodged there, undo the screws which hold the brushes, remove the fluff, and do the screws up again. Oiling the machine before knitweaving is also important. (See figure 61.)

Feeding the yarn by hand It's quite easy to feed the yarn by hand. Starting with the carriage at the right, loop the yarn over the right hand table clamp to anchor it securely. The guides on the carriage will be used, as before, but the yarn can simply be held just above the carriage with the left hand. The carriage is pushed across to the left as usual, using the right hand and letting the weaving yarn slip through the left hand fingers. The left hand only guides the yarn, it isn't meant to hold it. (See figure 43.) Once the carriage is across the needlebed, the yarn is allowed to drop down, taken out of the guide, then under the carriage, and brought out just above the right hand carriage guide, being held with the right hand while the carriage is operated with the left. Care has to be taken to guide the yarn in the proper way, and this may be easier with some machines than with others, but only experience will show you how to do it best. Once mastered, the method not only makes it simple to weave with several colours for one garment piece, it also overcomes the problem of textured yarns catching on parts of the yarn brake. It's possible to use balled weaving yarns without rewinding them because the knitting isn't too fast for smooth unwinding, and less yarn is needed for each row. Threading the yarn taken from the centre of a commercially wound ball through a wax disc smooths hairy or textured yarns.

Using weights The small claw weights provided with modern machines need to be used at the side edges when knitweaving; when using the holding position, it's a great help to have a few more of these weights to prevent the material riding up on the needlebed, which it has a tendency to do when you're using the fluffier weaving yarns. A good pull all along the row now and again can be helpful too.

Using the holding position Knitting back from the holding position may take a little practice. The needles from the holding position have to be brought back into just the right place. This varies with the make of the machine and you may have to practise to find just the right position on yours.

Casting on extra stitches Casting on after the main body of the piece has been started is quite easy, so long as you remember to bring the weaving yarn up *after* the extra stitches; if you don't, you get a loop and unsatisfactory knitting for the first few stitches.

Taking off the ribber It's much easier to knit-weave without the ribber, so take it off if you own a single bed machine with a ribber attachment.

Patterns using left out needles

The advantages of leaving some of the working needles in the A or non-working position were mentioned in Chapter 3. Thicker yarns can be used, lace and mock rib patterns can be made, and textured yarns are easier to knit with. However, as fewer needles, and consequently fewer stitches, will be available, the width of the fabric produced will be somewhat limited. It's worth considering a tuck stitch pattern to widen it. The simpler the pattern, the easier it will be to knit difficult yarns. But it's not only thick and textured yarns which benefit from tuck patterns with left out needles. A whole new spectrum of lace is provided by the judicious use of this device. Figure 41 is an example of a tuck lace pattern. What you arrange to do is to leave out needles in such a way that the tucking will create holes in the longer strands of yarn produced by the left out needles.

Figure 40 shows an effective mock cable. As every fourth needle is left in the non-working position many double knitting yarns can be used.

Once set up, tuck laces are very quick and easy to knit. The patterns stand out in relief, are very warm and flexible, and a large range of yarns – from the very fine to double knitting – can be used to make them. (See figure 103 and plate 8, facing p. 97.)

Patterns by punchcard

Designing your own punchcard patterns is one of the creative outlets of punchcard machine knitting. Some people are at a loss to know how to punch cards for left-out needles. The simplest method, to my mind, is to take a thick felt-tipped pen and a ruler. Rule down every column which is to represent a needle in the non-working position. You're now left with a punchcard on which to design your pattern. For example, if every alternate needle is in A position, you will have a 12-space card; if every fourth needle is in A position, you will have an 18-space card. The main thing to bear in mind is the need to align the punched card with the needles in the working position by relating them to the red line on the numbered side of the blank punchcard – this corresponds to the 0 mark on the needlebed. If

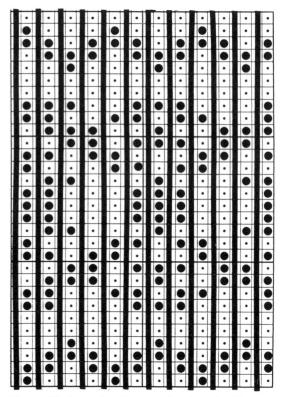

Figure 98 *A punchcard prepared and punched for using alternate needles*

needle number 1 on the right hand side of 0 is in the non-working position, the column corresponding to this must be ignored on the punchcard for design purposes; it can be left blank because it won't affect the needles in the working position. (See figure 98.)

If you're using alternate needles you can use any patterns which are repeats of 12 or factors of 12; that is, if they repeat every 2, 3, 4, 6 or 12 stitches. This means, for instance, that some fairisle patterns can be knitted in the thicker yarns. A card punched for some of the patterns used in figure 114 is given in figure 98. Many cards can be used as they are, simply by ignoring every other column.

Designing cards for tuck lace is slightly more difficult, because you need to consider not only the left out needle positions, but also the tucking needles. Figure 99 shows the punchcard used for the tuck lace T-shirt in plate 8, facing p. 97.

Using the same punchcard for many patterns
You may have noticed that I make use of the same punchcard for a variety of examples; this is to show just how versatile they are.

The mechanism which holds the card on a particular line can be used to try out a number of patterns, without going to the bother and expense of punching a card before you know you'd like to use the pattern. One or two lines will be quite enough for many of the tuck lace patterns. (See figure 99.)

Existing punchcards can be modified by holding some pattern rows for two or three carriage movements. The punchcard in Pattern 4 was adapted from Knitmaster basic card 16.

Patterns can be added to an existing card by clipping another card to it, then clipping the end of this one to the beginning of the first.

These suggestions are intended simply to get you started on creating your own fabric, on making what is in every sense your new material. You can find more advanced hand and machine knitting patterns and techniques in some of the books listed in the reading list at the end of this book. But you'll discover many new ways of using your needles or your knitting machine for yourself. Knitting in traditional ways is a satisfying craft. Inventing new fabrics is something of a satisfying art.

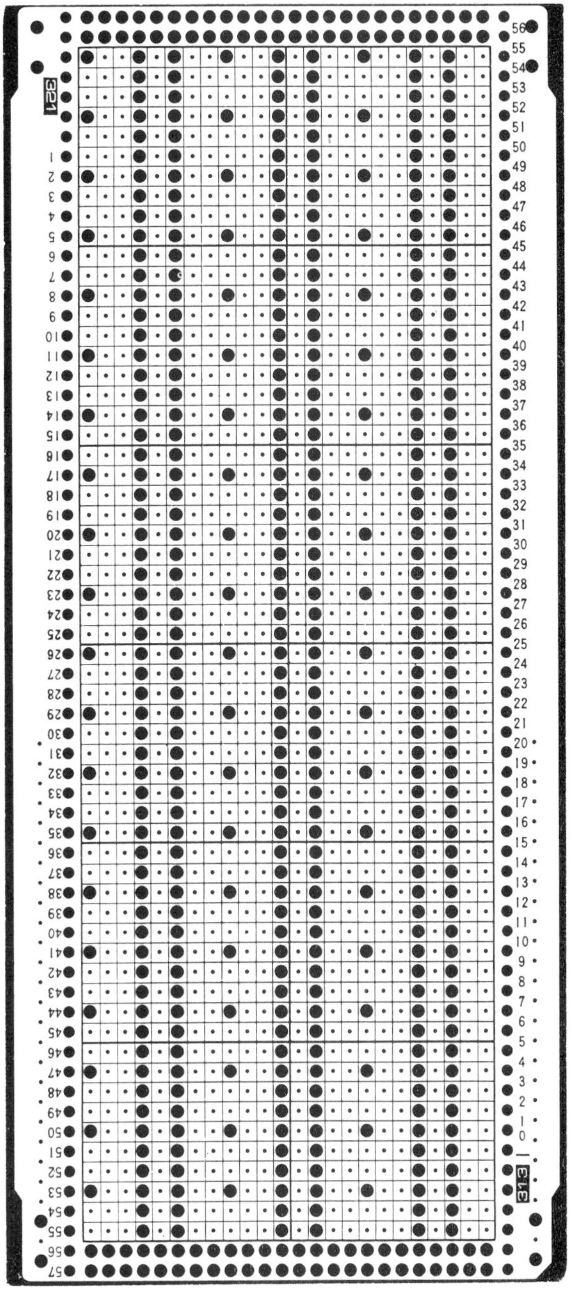

Figure 99 *The punchcard used for the tuck lace T-shirt in plate 8*

8 GETTING IT TOGETHER

It's all very well to have the tools, the raw materials, the right tensions and now the fabrics; but there's still a little more to do before an article can be made and used – the separate pieces must be adequately shaped, put together and 'finished'. This is true whether one merely sews in yarn-ends on a dish-cloth or applies the most sophisticated dressmaking techniques to fabrics produced by the metre or yard. If the beautiful new material is to be shown off to the best advantage, one needs to acquire some of the skills that will make this possible. This is a big subject, and it would take another book to do it justice; but I'm at least going to indicate simple ways in which you can show off your work; how these methods can be used to correct any knitting mistakes; and how, even for garments made of quite ordinary knitted fabric, completely individual knit-wear can be produced.

As it happens, one of the advantages of knitting is that some of the more arduous dressmaking steps can be left out; the knitted piece can be shaped while it's being worked, and there'll be no raw edges to consider. All one need do is assemble the garment pieces – often, but not necessarily, by sewing. Shaping and edging a garment piece as it's being knitted slows down the knitting process; nevertheless, it's often very worthwhile. Only you can decide whether it's worthwhile for you, and you may well choose to combine cut and sew with the traditional edging and shaping of knitted pieces. This will, no doubt, depend on what you're making, as well as on your personal preferences.

The patterns in this book are chosen to illustrate some of the ways in which one can easily produce well-fitting knitwear, together with suggestions for quick and simple ways of getting over common problems. Always see if you can think of short cuts for yourself, and don't be too worried about what looks 'right' for the right side. The 'wrong' side, even of a seam, often makes interesting patterns on its own. Why not put them to use?

Shaping garment pieces

Shaping is a nightmare for many knitters. Fortunately, many modern garments are made with the minimum of shaping, and the basic pattern given in Chapter 6 gives ample scope for a whole wardrobe of sweaters. However, even the best pattern has its limitations, and the other patterns in this book have been chosen to show further simple basic shapes which will give the least number of problems and yet produce worthwhile garments. The following techniques are all you need to make them up successfully.

Shaping while you knit

Basic shaping for garment pieces was discussed at the end of Chapter 6. Essentially, any shaping done at the edges of a piece of knitting presents no trouble for most people after a little practice. One only has to know how to increase and to decrease, and to keep a tally of the rows between such shapings. The trouble starts when shaping has to be done in the centre of a garment – at the neckline, for instance. Though cut and sew can solve this problem for light and medium weight fabrics, for thicker weights you may find it can become too cumbersome, or too wasteful of yarn; so it's better to look for other solutions.

Altering the tension, stitch or yarn

Shaping by altering the tension, stitch pattern or yarn was discussed in Chapter 7; this is a surprisingly helpful method for many garments. As this type of shaping is evenly spread across the fabric width, it's particularly useful for waist, neck-band and roll-collar shaping as well as for skirts and hats.

Elastic

A further simple but very useful device is to use elastic. Shirring elastic, a special type of thin elastic,

Figure 100 *Using elastic: a soft, wide elastic sewn to the eased waistline of a skirt will produce a snug fit and good stiffening*

can be used to make a well-fitting ribbed neckline. It can just as well be used on the ribbed cuffs of sleeves to make them tight enough, or to keep synthetic yarns in shape. But there's no reason why this type of elastic shouldn't be used at the waist of a sweater or dress, whatever the stitch pattern. The shirlastic can be threaded into the stitches so that it can't be seen from the 'right' side. The method will vary for each pattern, and it may need a little ingenuity to do it in the best way, but it can usually be done. The shirlastic may have to be used for several rows, and it may be wise to mark these rows by knitting in a cotton thread to help keep a straight line, but trial and error will soon show the best way for you.

Shirlastic can also be knitted in. Obviously, if there's a colour which exactly matches the yarn, a few rows of knitted elastic, suitably tensioned, can be substituted for the yarn. A simple fairisle pattern, say two stitches knitted in the yarn and two stitches in the tensioned shirlastic all along each row for several rows, will produce an excellent elastic piece very quickly; punch lace patterns can also be used. However, the disadvantage of these methods is that shirlastic doesn't last as long as most yarns, so that threading it into the fabric after knitting is usually a better method.

All other kinds of elastic can be pressed into service: narrow loom elastic for the cuffs and hems of blousons, wider types for waistbands, roll elastic for necklines . . .

Using a soft, wide elastic at the waist of a skirt can be an excellent idea; the waistline of the knitted piece can be eased and sewn to fit a piece of elastic cut to the exact waist size and, if the piece is wide enough, it will produce a snug fit and sufficient stiffening. (See figure 100.) It will also be comfortable to wear. If something doesn't quite fit, think

Figure 101 *A knitted-in hem; this automatically produces pattern contrast on the purl side of this tuck stitch fabric*

of shirlastic, or even of some other form of elastic. Then perhaps it will.

The holding position

Held stitches can often be used for easy shaping; some examples are given in the patterns, but this method can be exploited in all kinds of ways. The heel and toe shapings given in all machine instruction books can be adapted for making neat ends for, among other things, belts, collars and mittens. (See figure 101). Wide pierrot collars are easily shaped by knitting them sideways; zigzag patterns can be made, for example, to give unusual hemlines.

Horizontal darts are readily knitted by holding stitches, and the hemlines of skirts, dresses or even coats can easily be curved for a much-improved look as discussed in Chapter 7. Pattern 2 shows one way to make yokes by using the holding position. The pleats in the skirt shown in figure 102 are quickly made and don't add too much bulk. The shaped fronts of the waistcoat in figure 103 are also easily made.

Sideways knitting

Knitting sideways is a method which can be used to make neck shaping as simple as any side shaping, and Pattern 2 illustrates one way of working this out; there are many others.

Front bands for cardigans or jackets are also easily knitted by this method, and buttonholes for the bands are simple to space and knit. (See figure 6.)

Figure 102 *A mock-pleated skirt, with yoke shaped by the holding position*

Figure 103 *Tuck lace. Both sides of this pattern can be used by making the waistcoat reversible*

You need not, of course, knit the whole garment sideways; you can merely knit on the bands if you prefer.

Knitting downwards

Knitting down from the neck to the hem, rather than up from the hem, is a way of simplifying the neck shaping. Pattern 3 is knitted like this. The advantage is that one side of the neck can easily be knitted and then held in the holding position, or, perhaps more conveniently, held on a spare needle or taken off the machine until the other side has been worked. Psychologically, if nothing else, this method has the advantage that, if things go wrong, not much work has been done and it's quick to start again. But apart from that, it's easier to place a bold pattern in an aesthetically pleasing position – after all, the front neckline is where it shows most. And,

for punchcard knitting, there's no trouble about finding the right pattern line; you simply start at the chosen line for each side, and, when it's time to hook the first side back onto the machine, the right pattern line is automatically there.

It's true that finishing at the waist, hip or hemline may be a little harder than starting there, particularly if you like knitting-in a hem or starting on a ribber attachment; however, better to have to overcome these small difficulties than the greater ones often involved in pattern knitting a complicated neckline at the end of a garment piece.

Another advantage is that the length of a sweater, skirt or sleeve may be more easily adjusted, when fashion changes, or the wearer is a child who's grown, or if you simply got it wrong.

Finishing edges

Edges which are to be seamed to other edges don't need any special treatment; the seaming itself sees to that. It's the unseamed edges of a garment – at the waist or hipline of a sweater, the hem of a dress, the cuff of a sleeve, the armholes on a sleeveless garment, the necklines, the edges of collars – which often have pieces, called 'welts', knitted along them. The word suggests a strip of fabric somewhat thicker than that of the rest of the piece, and stitch patterns suitable for welts do, indeed, make thicker fabrics than stocking stitch. It's the 'welt' edges of garments made of fabrics which roll that need to have some thought given to them before they're made.

There are a number of solutions to the problem; some will have plain, unobtrusive and functional results, others will be easy to carry out, still others will produce eyecatching parts of the design. Which solution is chosen should depend on the article one's making, what it's intended for, and on the personality and skills of the knitter.

As the problem has to be considered in any case, why not make use of the solution to give garments a highly individual look? The appearance of almost any standard knitted article can be completely changed by considering how to make the welts imaginatively. A sports sweater can be turned into a dazzling evening garment by a change of yarn and by making the welts in a different way. Below are a few of many possible suggestions, simple enough for the beginner to handle. In effect, the welts often turn into finishing touches, usually called trimmings. Some need to be planned before the garment is made, but some can be added as an afterthought,

Figure 104 *Tuck stitch edging. A deep tuck will provide a machined edge quickly and simply*

either because the garment is to be used for a different purpose, or because fashions now include this particular idea.

Fabric roll

Using the fabric roll by allowing a certain roll-back, and regulating this by oversewing with blanket stitch or any other simple device, often makes an unusual, simple and decorative border. A deep tuck will provide a scalloped edge quickly and simply in machine knitting. (See figure 104.) Figure 41 shows that a tuck stitch can turn back on itself at the side edges very effectively.

Using stitch patterns

Knitted fabric has a great advantage over woven fabric; instead of having to face or hem the edges of garments, the stitch pattern can simply be changed to edging which is functional, good looking and easy to make. A number of the stitch patterns discussed in Chapters 2 and 3 are ideal for welts; in fact, many combinations of plain and purl stitches in the same row, or plain and purl knitted alternately for a few rows, will produce a non-curling fabric and can be used for edging. This means that single bed machines cannot produce welt stitches, but there is one exception: knitweave, if used in the right combination of backing yarn and weaving yarn, can make some excellent, though inelastic, welts. It may be necessary to finish off with one row of double crochet, but often even this can be dispensed with.

Hemming

A hem is made by turning material back on itself in some way and attaching that part to the main body of the piece. This not only gives a neat finish, it gives strength, firmness and weight to the edge of a garment, and is at the same time an effective anti-roll treatment. Fabrics made of fine yarns are often better hemmed; single bed work is easily hemmed and certain classical garments look better if they're finished in this way. Plate 1 (facing p. 72) shows a knitted hem at the waist, the cuffs and the neckline.

Again, there are many hems which can be made and used; a few suggestions are given in the patterns, but it's easy to think of others. A stitch pattern might, for instance, be used for the hem of a stocking stitch garment; the hem can be turned to whichever side seems more in keeping with the garment. A different colour could be used for the hem backing, and a stitch pattern chosen which allows the colour to show through for the rest of the hem. In order to make sure that the hems lie flat, it's helpful to use a tighter tension on the hem backing, or even to use fewer needles or stitches, particularly with synthetic yarns, to make sure the fabric stays flat and doesn't flute out.

Hems can be used for cardigan bands and borders, sleeve cuffs, waistbands, collars, piping and even casing. A little thought, a lot of possibilities.

Binding

A method of enclosing raw edges, called 'binding', is often used in dressmaking. Knitted fabric can be bound at a shaped edge even more easily, in the sense that, as there's no fraying in the shaped pieces, the edge need not be enclosed, but just hidden by some attractive material. This can be any – bought or made – braid or trimming, and can be attached by sewing or bonding on with the new materials available for this purpose. Bonding will stiffen the edges, and this can be useful for cardigan bands, for instance; but it can only be used for pressable yarns.

It's also possible to use knitted strips for enclosing the edges altogether. Bands of plain, patterned or bias knitting can be used, and many tuck stitches make delightful shell edgings.

Crochet

Crochet is a real help. Many people shrink from it because they think it's difficult and time consuming; actually it's neither. A basic row of single or double crochet worked round the unseamed edges is a useful way of getting borders to exactly the right length, and of evening up any irregularities due to complicated shaping or inexperienced knitting. Very often this is all you need to do, but, for special effects, stitch patterns and colours can now be added, and they won't show any irregular shapings. Buttonholes couldn't be easier; just use filet crochet. This can also be used to make casings for ribbon, laces or cording. Using attractive edging stitches, with the yarn doubled, is a good way to finish lace fabrics; the edging has more weight, and it's quicker to do. 'Add on' is especially easy in crochet. A garment can be transformed by adding borders in different colours, by using yarn threaded with beads, pearls or sequins, by working textured stitch patterns, and by crocheting onto the fabric as well as onto the edges to form raised designs. . . . Use your own judgement; don't be afraid to experiment. You can always undo the crochet, but if you don't try something new, you're not very likely to produce something new. (See plate 6, facing p. 96.)

It really is a pity to get into a rut about edgings; as I said at the beginning, the work has to be done in any case, so why not use it to form a significant part of the design, or even to be its main feature? Make bold use of the welts; the basic knitting can be as plain and quick as you like. Your time can be spent creatively, and inexpensively, by concentrating on the trimmings.

Forming attachments

Whatever method you've used to knit a garment, sooner or later there's a pile of pieces which have to be attached to each other. A certain amount of sewing can be avoided, but eventually some will have to be done either by hand or machine.

Preparation for sewing

Should the pieces be pressed or steamed before seaming them? I think that depends on whether they've been knitted to be used for cut and sew or whether they've been shaped while knitting.

Preparing cut and sew A counsel of perfection would be to wash, dry and press all fabric before cutting out. That's the method recommended for unshrunk fabric bought by the metre (yard). However, domestically knitted lengths usually start and end with open loops, and washing is, to my mind, too drastic a treatment. I think it's better to pin matching pieces together, right sides inside, and then press or steam the pieces on both sides. Single pieces can be folded back on themselves, as long as the fold isn't pressed into the fabric. The temperature of the iron must be suited to the fibre content of the yarn which was used to knit the lengths. Many stitch patterns should be steamed and not pressed; otherwise it's all too easy to flatten stitch patterns whose charm lies in their raised effect, or to ruin the elasticity of ribbing.

Steaming will shrink a fabric made of unstabilised yarn, release the tension due to yarn and knitting, and set the loops so that they're not so liable to run when the shapes are cut out.

Preparing shaped pieces If the pieces are already shaped, I think it's much better not to use an iron. It's very easy to distort small pieces of knitwear when they're being pressed. Of course, the tension swatch should have been washed or steamed, as I explained in Chapter 6. I prefer to assemble the pieces as they are. Once the garment has been seamed, it's simple to wash the whole thing and smooth it into the correct shape, to dry and set to exactly the right size.

Washing knitted fabric Knowing how to wash knitted fabric is a great help. Once you know how to do it your knitwear will have a very long life and you can save yourself the trouble of pressing. The following guidelines can be used for any yarn, and, in my opinion, give the best finish to a beautifully crafted garment.

There are four main points: use lukewarm water; completely dissolve the cleansing agent in the water; support the knitting from underneath so that it doesn't stretch when lifted as a wet mass; and spin out the water on the lowest available spin, or squeeze the knitting dry between towels.

A newly knitted garment needs only a few drops of fabric softener or cleansing agent, but for any other garment I completely dissolve the agent in lukewarm water in one side of my double sink; then I ease the knitting into the solution, allowing it to soak while I fill the other sink. After that I swish the article gently about, squeezing the solution through it with my hands. I lift it – supporting it from underneath – out of the cleansing solution into the first rinsing water. I change the rinsing water two or three times and add a fabric softener to a last rinse. The short, slow spin on my washing machine is ideal to get the right stage for the setting process. Any flat surface, even a towel-covered floor, can be used to *smooth* the garment into the correct shape, first on the back, then carefully turning it over, on the front. Ribbed welts are pulled into their tightest shape, hems smoothed flat, stitch patterns adjusted. Avoid sunlight in the drying area, as it affects the colours. Once dry, the garment is smoothly set into the shape and size it will have for the rest of its life, apart from minimal fibre shrinkage. Oil spun yarn can be scoured very simply by dissolving two tablespoons of washing soda in two gallons of fairly hot water, as I mentioned in Chapter 5. The combination of oil and soda forms soap, and will extract the oil much more efficiently than detergent. The result will be a beautifully fluffy garment.

For the professional look, you can always press the garment after washing, using whatever setting on the iron is suited to the fibre content of the yarn.

Seaming

There are quite a few ways of making seams to join knitted pieces; which one is used depends not only on personal preference, how much time you have, your particular skills, and the machines at your disposal, but also on the particular yarns and patterns you employ. Garments knitted in fine yarns will often need different seams from those knitted in medium or thick yarns; textured or fancy yarns set different problems from plain ones; complicated patterns with thick relief stitches will need different treatment from delicate laces; reversible garments call for other solutions than those used for single sided ones. There is, then, no point in laying down hard and fast rules. All I can do is make suggestions which may help to guide you to a particular solution; I think it's essential to try out various methods and then decide what you like for yourself. There's absolutely no point in using a particular sewing stitch because someone else says it's a good idea.

Figure 105 *The seam produced by knitting a raglan sleeve onto the previously knitted back and front of a garment*

On the other hand, don't stay in a rut; if you come across a new way of making up, try it out in case it's better than any of the ones you've tried so far.

Knitting in and knitting on is often a good way to avoid a seam altogether. Raglan sleeves, for instance, can be attached to the previously knitted back and front of a garment by knitting them from the neck down, and picking up edge stitches from the back and front as you knit. (See figure 105.) Pattern 1 shows how a crew collar can be knitted on from the body quite simply. Shoulder seams can be ignored or replaced by darts by starting and finishing the body of a garment at the waist. (See figure 106.) Knitting cardigans or jackets from side to side makes it possible to eliminate side seams. Collars, cuffs, neckbands and hems can all be added by picking up stitches from the appropriate edges and then knitting the piece on these. Once you're aware of the possibilities, you'll find that there are many opportunities for avoiding seams.

Knitting on a sleeve head It's possible to pick up the stitches for a sleeve head from the armhole edges and knit downwards. (See figure 42.) For a shaped sleeve head, pick up all the stitches you need for the sleeve width from the armhole edges. Put all but the central stitches in holding and knit the held stitches in, row by row, according to the pattern. The sleeve will be attached neatly and quickly and the seam will be elastic.

Casting off Though casting off is a slow and tedious way to finish work on a knitting machine, it does have one or two things to recommend it, as it can be used as a seam-making device as well. Following the method given in Chapter 3, the cast-off row can have any length you choose, and the yarn can be strengthened by adding a buttonhole thread in an appropriate colour. Shirring elastic can be used instead of yarn to produce a completely elastic finish.

Making a shoulder seam by casting off To make a neat, non-stretch shoulder seam for a garment knitted from waist to neck, hold the stitches to shape the shoulders and finish the work with open

Figure 106 *Replacing a shoulder seam by a dart*

loops. Put the right sides of both pieces together, and put two stitches, one from each shoulder, on each machine needle, or alternately on a knitting needle. Knit these two stitches together all across the row, either by hand or machine. Cast off at the same time or on the next row, strengthening the casting-off yarn with buttonhole thread and adjusting the length of the row so that the seam is precisely as you want it. (See figure 77.)

Attaching a collar by casting off This method is particularly useful for machine knitting. Knit the collar, starting at the outside edge and finishing at the neck edge. Leave this open-looped edge on the machine. Work out how to set the collar correctly and pick up stitches from the edges of the garment to which the collar is to be attached. Using one stitch from the collar, one from the edge, knit these two stitches together across the row. Even a closed curve neckline can be used if you pick up edge stitches and cast off as you go. Try shirlastic as the casting-off yarn for a snug fit.

This method can also be used for cuffs, neck-

Figure 107 *Tubular or hemmed bands are easily attached to a garment by back stitching through the open loops*

bands and other small pieces. Whenever a pattern calls for casting off, check to see if you can make use of it for a seam.

Finishing with open loops Casting off in pattern is a good way to finish many welt edges, but I don't like it for finishing edges to be seamed. My method is to thread a piece of knitting yarn through the open loops, allowing plenty of yarn so that the edge stays flexible.

The advantages are that there's no ugly ridge to hide in the seam, the fabric stays completely flexible, and it's ready for quick sewing by whatever method. The loops are stopped from running, and in most cases the threaded yarn won't show. If you wish to remove it later, substitute nylon cord or a smooth, strong cotton.

Attaching tubular or hemmed bands Knitted bands with open loops, made on double or single bed machines, are often attached to garment edges by 'sandwiching' the edge between the two sides of the band. Back stitch is used through the open loops, first on one, then on the other side of the fabric. (See figure 107.) This makes an excellent, neat and reversible finish, though there are three layers of fabric at the overlap, and this needs to be considered.

Figure 108 *Grafting two pieces of jersey together*

Grafting A yarn–threaded needle or small bodkin can be used to join together two knitted pieces with open loops. The stitch pattern can be followed by weaving in and out of the loops appropriately, and figure 108 shows the method for plain jersey. The method can be adapted for many stitch patterns.

Semi-grafting A yarn-threaded needle can be used to join a knitted piece with open loops to the main sections of a garment. This is particularly useful for joining sections of horizontal and vertical knitting. The same effect is obtained in hand and single bed knitting by picking up stitches from an edge and knitting on these loops, as already mentioned, but for double bed knitting this would be too awkward.

Latch-up This is a particularly good way of making reversible seams: all shaping is done two or three stitches in from the edges of a garment; the first and last stitches on the cast-off row are dropped, giving an edging of loops on both selvedges. (See figure 109.) Using a latchet tool or crochet hook, the loops can be latched-up in ones or twos, to provide an excellent, decorative, flat seam.

The raglan sleeves in Pattern 3 are shaped by increasing one stitch at the beginning of every row. Latch-up was used on the loops formed by these increases – made at the fabric edges. Plate 3 (facing p. 73) shows a seam.

Crochet It's very easy to crochet through two thicknesses of fabric, using two edge stitches as the base. Single or double crochet stitches can be used, and the slight ridge showing on one side can be used as part of the design. (See figure 96.) A flat seam can also be made, by taking the crochet hook out of the yarn, putting it through the second edge and then crocheting on, as shown in figure 110. Fancy stitches can be inserted for a lacy seam, and this can be a very effective addition to garment design. The seam is reversible.

Hand sewing up It's helpful to know how to do a few of the traditional hand sewing stitches.

Back stitch is very useful, and is made by putting the right sides of two fabric pieces together, then sewing as shown in figure 53. Be sure to sew well inside any cast-off edges, otherwise you're left with an ugly ridge on the right side. It's a good stitch for tailored or lace garments, and can be adapted for sewing zips invisibly by making the top stitches very small. These are then called stab stitches.

Mattress stitch is made by weaving the yarn from one side to the other of fabrics placed edge to edge, their right sides facing you as you sew. If worked one or two stitches inside the selvedge, there'll be a virtually invisible seam on the front of the garment and faults at the edge can be hidden in a fairly thick ridge at the back. If worked right at the edge, a flat, reversible seam is produced. Fairisle and striped patterns are easy to match up because you're working from the right side. (See figure 111.)

Flat or oversew stitch is made by placing the pieces of fabric edge to edge, running the index

Figure 109 *Preparing for latch up. The left side shows shaping done one stitch in from the side edge. The right side shows the loops formed at the side edge by dropping the first stitch on the last row and pulling out the loops*

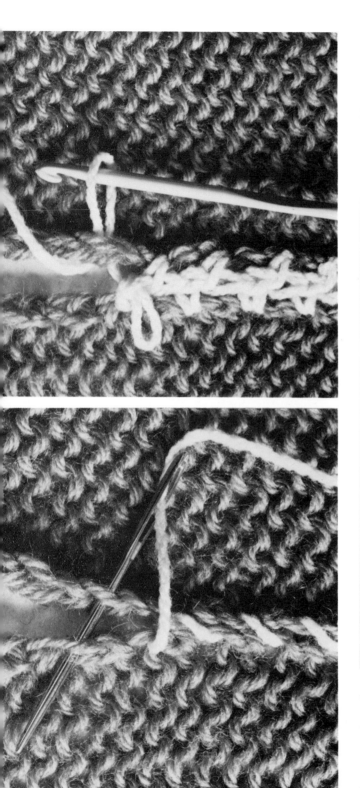

Figure 110 *Joining two pieces of fabric with a flat crochet seam* (above left)

Figure 111 *Mattress stitch* (above)

Figure 112 *Flat or oversew stitch* (left)

Figure 113 *A wavy seam produced by incorrect machine stitching*

finger of the left hand between the pieces as you sew, and over-stitching corresponding edge stitches. This is a good stitch for ribbed welts and reversible garments or for garments made in very chunky yarns. (See figure 112.)

Mending a pulled thread If you pull a thread in knitwear, don't make a knot and cut off the excess. Take a thick, blunt ended needle and use it to tease the yarn gently back into its original position in the row. It's not difficult, but it can be hard to see what's going on. Pull lightly on the snagged yarn – you will then see the movement and where to adjust the yarn much more easily. Teach the rest of the family how to do it; you'll find that they'll be careful not to snag their knitwear when they know what a tedious job it is to repair it – *and* that the job is theirs! Such repairs can be made quite invisible, and are, I think, very worthwhile.

Machine sewing up Apart from the special link and interlock machines already mentioned, domestic sewing machines are useful for seaming knitted fabrics. As I said in Chapter 4, it's possible to use an ordinary straight stitch machine by using the longest stitch and a light tension, but when the fabric stretches the stitch may break. A narrow zigzag stitch, made with a special attachment or a swing needle, will give a more stretchable but less continuous seam. Stretch stitch machines make very adequate seams; some are able to overcast and make a straight seam in one go. Some skill is needed to get the correct tension, otherwise you may get a wavy seam as shown in figure 113. Mistakes made using stretch stitches can only be repaired by cutting apart and starting again. This can be done, but it's unnerving!

Machine sewing is particularly useful for cut and sew work, especially if stretch stitches are available. Knitweave, too, benefits because the overcasting flattens the otherwise rather bulky seam. Lace fabric can be made to look very neat, and of course all the sewing is quicker than by hand. (See figure 53.)

Fastenings

Finally, your garment may need fastenings. These are often the very first thing people notice about a garment, so which ones you choose matters. There's a very large choice of plastic buttons at the haberdashery counters. These buttons are light, serviceable and cheap, but you might well like something more individual to set off your original work. Specialist shops and large department stores do have some splendid fastenings in bone, mother of pearl, various metals and wood. Many of these would make excellent choices, but they are, unfortunately, expensive.

Still, there are alternatives. One is to make your own buttons by, for instance, crocheting round curtain rings and criss-crossing the centre with sewing stitches. There are button moulds which can be covered in your own crafted materials – perhaps by using up the tension swatch. And there's another useful method. You can buy acrylic or pva paints and painting medium. These are waterproof, and can be painted onto any plain wooden buttons – very easily and cheaply bought. The medium can be matt, semi-matt and glossy, and gives you the opportunity to make the buttons washproof and to use the natural look of the wood. Use the paints if you want a colour to match your garment.

Reversible fastenings Tie fastenings, made of crochet or cord, are a good way to fasten reversible clothes. Chunky buttons, sewn at the edge of the garment as in Pattern 3, zips with tapes hidden by bonded braids, wrap-over styles and separate clips are all adaptable. You can also sew buttons together through the buttonband; though the fastening will be the 'wrong' way on one side, this seems to me a minor drawback; after all, men traditionally wear garments fastened one way, women another. There's no important difference that I can spot!

Belts are easy to make or buy. Leather contrasts well with knitwear, crocheted rings joined together are versatile and slimming. Threading the ribbed tie-belt through the weaving has given a new look to Pattern 2. (See figure 120 and plate 6, facing p. 96.)

Accessories made of pottery, particularly belts and necklaces, are great enhancers of chunky knitwear. You may have a friend who makes pottery; why not ask him or her to make some accessories for you? The necklace in plate 1 (facing p. 72) is handmade pottery.

So now you're ready to put it all together. You need enthusiasm to start with, you need to invest a certain amount of money in the tools and the raw materials, you need time to acquire the skills to use the tools and materials, and you need to learn how to put together the fabric pieces you have so carefully learned to craft. All these things are important, but perhaps the most important – often the most neglected – is the last one. How you put the pieces together makes all the difference to the garment's look.

Your knitting may be perfect, your machine the most modern and automatic, your trimmings expensive and tasteful, your pattern or design original; but if you don't finally combine all these parts into a harmonious, pleasing and individual whole you won't enjoy the result. Give yourself the chance to enjoy it by taking trouble with this last, and often crucial, stage; and remember, mistakes in the knitted pieces can be corrected. Though this last part can seem the hardest, it's also the one that allows for the greatest originality. Don't throw away those beautifully crafted pieces because your first attempt at assembling them didn't work out. Try to fit them together again, perhaps in a different way. You *can* make something – and something worthwhile. Learn from your mistakes, they're often the most valuable lessons you'll have. Putting a sleeve in upside down *can* lead to an original idea for a design; using up those unlikely scraps of yarn *can* give you one of the most individual garments in your wardrobe. Turn the pieces round. Combine them in a variety of ways. Leave one out. Try to make something less ambitious with the rest. Eventually you'll come up with something of which you'll be proud to say: 'I made that. No, I didn't use a pattern. I worked it out myself.'

9 PERMUTATIONS ON A PATTERN

I'm sure that by now you'll be keen to work out your own patterns. I've written up four basic ones as examples. They can all be knitted by hand or machine and are illustrated in the colour plates. These simple patterns can be adapted to make similarly knitted but quite different looking clothes, and several permutations are suggested in each case. As I stressed in Chapter 6, size is a very individual matter; the size given is simply that of the illustrated garment. You can judge from that whether you'd like your own garments to be relatively longer, wider, with deeper cuffs or with any of the other variations which will make your clothes right for you.

The stitch pattern charts are given as 24 stitch repeats to serve a dual purpose. They can be used as charts for hand or non-automatic machine knitting by reading the thick blobs as one stitch or colour and the dots as another. Knitters using a 24-space punchcard machine can simply copy and punch the charts onto a blank punchcard or adapt a card they already have, but they must remember to start the pattern on the appropriate row for their make of machine. If your machine has a different way of patterning, or a punchcard using more or fewer spaces, you'll have to work out how to adapt a particular chart for that machine or, better, make up a more appropriate one.

The cast on and cast off methods are only specified if they're important for the particular pattern. Just use what you find most congenial, but remember to make the cast off loose enough.

It's necessary to set the row counter to 0 and the punchcard or any other patterning device to the correct row before starting to knit each garment piece.

The following list of abbreviations will help when jotting down patterns:

A, B, C, etc	contrast colours
alt	alternate
beg	beginning
carr	carriage
col	colour
cm	centimetre, centimetres
dec	decrease
dc	double crochet
foll	following
gm	gramme, grammes
HP	holding position, held stitches
in	inch, inches
inc	increase
KM	knitting machine
K	knit (in the sense of work, not necessarily knitting plain across the row)
L	left
LHS	left hand side
M	main colour
no, nos	number, numbers
N	needle
NWP	non-working position
O	centre of needlebed on KM
R	right
RHS	right hand side
RC	row counter
st, sts	stitch, stitches
st-st	stocking stitch
T	tension
tog	together
WP	working position
W	knitweave

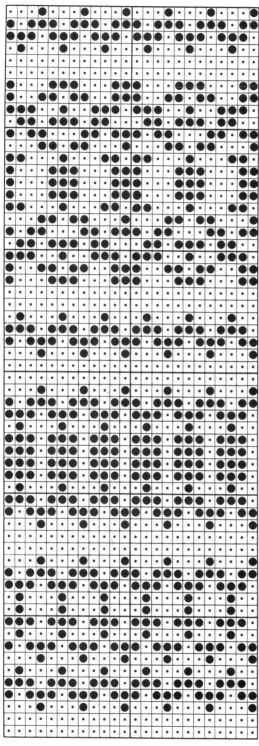

Figure 114 *The fairisle pattern used in Chapter 6, punched on a 24-space punchcard*

Pattern 1 – The basic sweater

The pattern is for a drop-sleeved, crew-necked sweater and a matching scarf knitted in an adaptation of some traditional fairisle stitch patterns. It's suitable for both men and women, and for children of any age. (See plate 1, facing p. 72, and figure 75.)

Materials Three separate strands of yarn are used. 200 gm (7 oz) of a medium thickness (2/10s) oiled Shetland wool, M, is used for the background and the welts, and the contrast colour A is made by doubling two strands, 75 gm (2½ oz) of each, of different coloured Kyoto, a mohair mixture yarn available from Silverknit. The scarf will need 125 gm (4½ oz) of M and 100 gm (3½ oz) of each of the two Kyoto colours. By using two strands of different coloured yarns for A, a mock multi-colour fairisle is easily and quickly made. Beginners might find knitting with a doubled yarn harder than knitting with a plied yarn; in that case simply use a second colour yarn of the same thickness as M. A random-dyed yarn will also give you a mock-fairisle.

Measurements

Chest 90 cm (35½ in.)
Body length from shoulder 62 cm (24½ in.)
Body length from top of shoulder 65·5 cm (25¾ in.)
Underarm seam 42 cm (16½ in.)
Cuff 7 cm (2¾ in.)
Armhole 20 cm (8 in.)

Scarf:

Length 185 cm (73 in.) without fringe
Width doubled back 27 cm (10½ in.)

Stitch patterns The hems and crew neckband are knitted in stocking stitch, the sleeve cuffs in 2×1 mock rib. The main parts of the sleeves and body pieces are in bands of fairisle separated by rows of stocking stitch in M, as shown in chart 1, figure 114. Hand knitters should read odd rows purl from R to L and even rows knit from L to R, and add appropriate first and last stitches. It may be necessary to disconnect A from feeder 2 on some automatic machines when knitting the stockinet rows.

Tension The garment was knitted on a punchcard machine. T8 produced a tension of 27 sts and 29 rows to 10 cm (4 in.), measured over the fairisle pattern. The hems and mock ribs were knitted at T6. Hand knitters should find 3 mm Ns (US size 2) approximately right for the hems and 4 mm Ns (US size 5) right for the main parts. A double rib worked on 3 mm Ns (US size 2) should make satisfactory cuffs.

Scarf

	RC
Cast on 145 sts in M, using 4 mm Ns (US size 5) or T8.	
K in pattern according to the chart for 536 rows	537
If you're using the scarf as a tension swatch, mark it as given in Chapter 6.	
Cast off *loosely* in M	

Finishing Fold the scarf lengthways and seam the edges together, using a half stitch seam allowance from both sides.

With wrong sides together, set the seam down the centre of one side. Join the two fabric sections at top and bottom by making a fringe with a crochet hook through both together. This holds the seam in place as well as finishing the scarf.

Wash and smooth into shape, and allow to dry. Measure the tension swatch and pull out the markers.

Sweater

Back and front alike
All methods

	RC
Cast on 121 sts on 4 mm Ns (US size 5) or T8	1
K 23 rows on 3 mm Ns (US size 2) or T6	24
Change to 4 mm Ns (US size 5) or T8 and pattern knitting	
K 16 rows	40
Form hem by picking up the sts from the cast-on row. Continue in pattern to 140 rows	140
Mark both edge sts for underarm	
K 58 rows	198
Put the last 3 Ns or sts at the end of each of the next 14 rows in HP	212
Bring 3 Ns or sts from HP to WP at the end of each of the next 14 rows	226
Cast off *loosely* in M over all Ns or sts	

Alternative for hand or double bed knitting
After row 198

	RC
Change to 3 mm Ns (US size 2) or T3/4 and 2×2 rib	
Put the last 3 sts or Ns at the end of each of the next 14 rows in HP	212
Cast off over all sts in rib	

Knit another body section in the same way

Sleeve
Hand and double bed knitting

Cast on 109 sts, using 3 mm Ns (US size 2) or the usual cast on tension for your machine	1

K for 25 rows, using a suitable rib or other welt st, using 3 mm Ns (US size 2) or T3/4	26

Single bed knitting

Put 107 Ns in WP	
Push every 3rd N to NWP	
Cast on in M over the remaining Ns and K 1 row at T6	1
K 48 rows	49
Bring forward the Ns previously put in NWP and one extra needle on both LHS and RHS (109 Ns)	
Hook the cast on row sts over these Ns, spacing them evenly so that there are 2 for every group of 3 and so that there's a st on each empty N	
Change to T8 and K 1 row	50
Reset row counter to 0 and start pattern knitting	

All methods

K 122 rows according to the chart or using a punchcard, on 4 mm (US size 5) Ns or T8.	122
Cast off *loosely* in M	

Knit another sleeve in the same way.

Finishing Slip stitch the hem in place on the wrong side of the neckline.

Join the sloping edges to form the shoulder seams.

Sew the cast-off edge of the sleeves between the markers on the back and the front.

Join the side and underarm seams in one operation.

Wash and smooth into shape, and allow to dry.

Permutations

I have listed below a number of simple pattern permutations to show how easy it is to get a completely different-looking garment without having to acquire more knitting know-how. You can, of course, use similar methods for the other patterns, and you will, I'm sure, discover many more possibilities for yourself.

Scarf

I like to double my fairisle scarves to enclose the floats and to make them really warm. Rib stitches would make narrower, thicker fabrics and many other hand and machine stitch patterns produce very good reversible wide scarves or stoles. Most patterns made by hand or on a double bed machine, and some single bed patterns, won't need any finishing at all along the edges, but, for those that do, choose any of the methods given for finishing edges in Chapter 8. The ends can be hemmed, fringed, finished in a crochet stitch, or simply left as they are and the scarf casually knotted.

A garment known as a 'shrug' is made in much the same way as a scarf, the only difference being that one starts and finishes with a tight cuff, made by any method. The cuffs are seamed, and the seam continued for about 10 cm (4 in.). Shrugs are best made a little wider and shorter than the scarf pattern given here: 140 cm (55 in.) long and 65 cm ($25\frac{1}{2}$ in.) wide are good proportions. The garment can be worn as an evening wrap, as a bed-jacket or for casual wear, depending on the stitch pattern and the yarn used. You might like to use it as a pattern/tension swatch for an evening dress, for instance.

Sweater

Sleeves The sweater can be varied very easily by making simple changes to the sleeves. Perhaps the simplest is to vary the sleeve length; make the underarm seam only 15 cm (6 in.) long and you have a short-sleeved sweater or oversweater. Leave off the cuff and knit a few rows in M to make a hem, and you have a quite different look. Knit the sleeve downwards and you not only change many stitch patterns, you can easily make a tight cuff by knitting two stitches together all along the row before starting the cuff; the length, of course, is as adjustable as before. Give the sleeve a different look by using some other welt stitches, either wide or narrow. A two-sided fabric is easily given interesting welts by hemming so that the reverse pattern shows as a contrast. (See figure 101.)

For a tapered sleeve, still with the same straight sleeve head, you need only refer to the method given in Chapter 6.

Neckline A simple, straight hem finish is the quickest to make; the shoulders are seamed just far enough to allow a slit which goes over the head easily. If the hem stands away from the body, just thread elastic into it to keep it neat.

A variation of the shallow crew neck given in the pattern instructions is to knit more rows and decrease one stitch only at the beginning or end of each row until you have the width of opening you'd like. Now reverse the process until you're back to the same number of stitches you started with. This can be done by using the stitches in holding for a neat shoulder seam, and the facing can be turned inside

out for a stitch pattern contrast with the main body. The same principle can be used to knit the neck in a rib pattern, either by hand or on a double bed machine. There's no need to make a facing for this version, as the ribbing will be strong enough on its own.

When working on a double bed machine, this sort of neck shaping is often quicker to work by knitting downwards from the neck. Cast on roughly one-third of the stitches needed for the chest size and choose a suitable rib stitch. Now increase one stitch at the beginning of each row until you have the number of stitches needed for the chest width. Either continue to knit a number of rows in the rib, for an easy yoke, or change to the main pattern.

This method can be extended to make a roll-type collar. Cast on about two-thirds of the chest width stitches. Knit 14–20 rows. Decrease one stitch at the end of the next 14–20 rows. Knit 20 rows straight. Change to a tighter tension, and knit straight for 20 rows. Now increase at the beginning of each row until you have the number of stitches needed for the main body. This is a very easy way to get a turned over roll collar without the usual trouble of rounding out the front neck and knitting a separate collar. (See figures 5 and 6.)

Body Changing the yarn and stitch pattern will, of course, make the sweater seem like quite a different garment. Knitting downwards changes the look of many patterns, but knitting sideways gives scope for even greater variations. (See figure 87.) Neck shaping is easy on sideways knitted garments, so you can vary the neckline without much trouble.

As with the sleeves, a plain body can make use of unusual welts, possibly in several colours, to give a different look and to use up spare yarn. The sweater can be shortened to end at the waist, with a ribbed welt to hold it in; it can be lengthened to make it into a tunic, possibly worn with a belt; tapered towards the waist and then out again to give a fitted look; made wider and threaded at hem and cuff for a blouson look – figure 115 shows a reversible blouson made to this pattern. The only change is a shaped neckline, which can be made by cut and sew or by using the holding position if you're not knitting sideways.

Leaving out the sleeves entirely is the way to a whole new series of garments. In the first place, you need only finish the armhole edges in an appropriate way to have a tabard. Tabards are often fastened at the side, and left open towards the hem, with perhaps a belt to cinch the waist. Make them a little

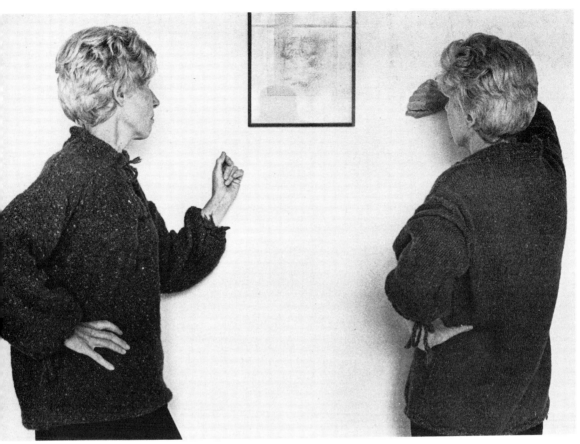

Figure 115 *A reversible blouson made in a punch lace pattern using two fine yarns*

wider to wear over sweaters as well as shirts.

If you're up to dividing the work, do so at around the armhole of the front; it's very easy to provide yourself with a V-neck by simply turning back lapels, crocheting or stitching them down as you wish. (See figure 116.)

Divide the front into two equal rectangles, and you have the pieces for a casual waistcoat or bolero, depending on the length. Increase the length and weight, and you have a poncho coat. (See figure 116.) Turn back a lapel, or shape the neckline. Gather the shoulder line for a flared body. Add fastenings at neck and waist, between neck and waist, or use a zip along the whole length. Each will have a different effect.

Batwing shapes can be made from two long rectangles: knit two the same size, sew up and leave openings for the neck and waist. Now add appropriate welts. Using the same size rectangles, divide one in two, vertically, knit the parts separately

and shape the neck a little, and you have the pieces for a batwing cardigan. Knit separate rectangles for the neckband, cuffs and welts. You won't find it difficult to adapt this to a tapered sleeve version. (See figure 117.)

Plate 3 (facing p. 73) shows a duffle coat knitted on the same principle: the body sections are slightly tapered below the waist to give a better shape, and the neckline has been rounded. The hood/collar is made by using the holding position.

Using rectangles for soft furnishings

As I said before, the rectangular shape can be used to make all kinds of soft furnishings for the home. Bath mats, for instance, can be quickly knitwoven using a cotton for the backing yarn with a thick cotton yarn woven into this for absorbency and resistance to wash and wear. Single colour dyeing and tie and dye give quick and easy colour variations for all-white mats.

The tuck lace settings can produce some very exotic-looking lace curtains or room dividers,

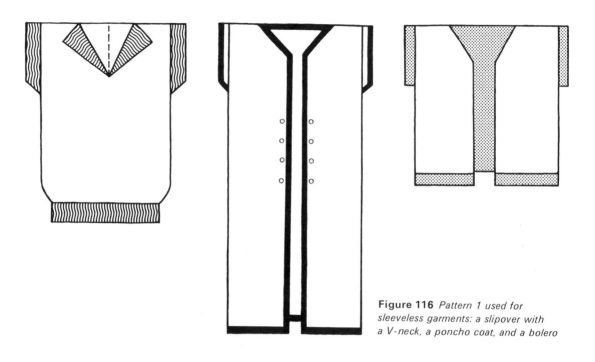

Figure 116 *Pattern 1 used for sleeveless garments: a slipover with a V-neck, a poncho coat, and a bolero*

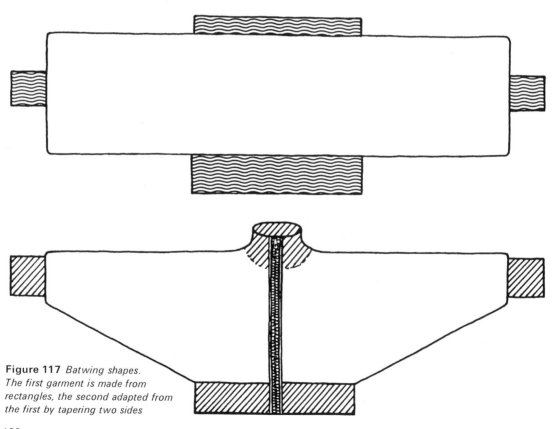

Figure 117 *Batwing shapes. The first garment is made from rectangles, the second adapted from the first by tapering two sides*

though they need to be carefully hung and weighted to look their best. Why not try out some of the more exotic yarns and materials by making yourself a wall-hanging? Start and finish with a narrow hem, and your piece will be easy to hang on any spare wall space by threading a rod through top and bottom and attaching some picture cord to the top one. This type of hanging will almost certainly 'drop' after a time, but the wooden rods will help to keep it flat.

Place mats are another idea for the beginner; they're useful for trying out stitch patterns. Why not a different knitweave or fairisle pattern for each member of the family, using the same colours and thickness of yarn? Make them reversible or double them for hiding floats and inserting heat-proof material.

If you feel really ambitious you can tackle curtains. These take a lot of time and yarn, but look well, particularly in simple knitweave patterns.

Pattern 2 – The yoked jacket

This drop-sleeved, yoked jacket with a flared body and a two-way collar is very easy to wear. It will suit women of any age, and is unusual in that the garment, illustrated in plate 2 (facing p. 72), will fit chest sizes 80 to 100 cm (32 to 40 in.); the mock pleats contract or expand as necessary. The underarm seam and body length are easily adjustable.

Whereas pattern 1 used permutations on the rectangle, pattern 2 uses permutations on the holding position. The basic concept is very simple and known to all machine knitters, though not as popular with hand knitters. Knit over all the stitches for some of the rows, but only some of the stitches for other rows. This leaves 'stitches in holding' for hand knitters, needles in the holding position for machine knitters. The pattern refers to both as HP.

If you vary the stitch pattern, the yarn thickness, the colours, or any combination of these, you can produce surprisingly varied garments with essentially the same simple pattern discussed in Chapter 6. Yokes and mock pleats appear automatically – there are no difficult shapings, and the result is a most accommodating fabric, suitable for both young and old, slim and not so slim.

Materials 120 gm ($4\frac{1}{2}$ oz) Falcon 2-ply Richmond was used as M, with 200 gm (7 oz) of random-dyed, poodle acrylic, Lister Poodle 1, used as the weaving yarn A. The jacket can easily be made using any combination of fine and thick yarns for knitting and knitweaving. An alternative would be to knit the long rows in a thick yarn, changing to a much finer yarn for the shortened rows. This method is much quicker for hand knitting, and will give the same mock pleat effect. There are 11 buttons.

Measurements
Chest 80–100 cm (32–40 in.)
Back yoke width 36 cm (14 in.)
Body length from top of shoulder 58 cm (23 in.)
Underarm seam 29 cm ($11\frac{1}{2}$ in.)
Cuff 13 cm (5 in.)
Armhole 21 cm ($8\frac{1}{2}$ in.)

Stitch pattern The whole garment is based on a 12 row pattern repeat. This is worked by knitweaving, using chart 2 (figure 118), across all the stitches for 8 rows, putting the required number of stitches in holding on the LHS of the face or 'right' side of the fabric, and knitting 4 rows over the remaining stitches. The Ns or sts in holding are then brought back into work. This is abbreviated to 'bring HP to WP' in the pattern instructions. The 'right' side faces the machine knitter as it comes off the machine, and is the purl side for the hand knitter.

Tension The illustrated garment was knitted on a punchcard machine. T6 produced a tension of 24 stitches and 37 rows to 10 cm (4 in.) over the knitwoven section. 3·25 mm Ns (US size 3) should produce a similar tension for hand knitters.

Jacket

The sleeves are knitted sideways. The body pieces are knitted as one section, with stitches cast off and on to form the armholes.

Sleeve
	RC
Cast on 100 sts in M on 3·25 mm (US size 3)	
Ns or T6	1
K 1 row	2
W 8 rows	10
Put 30 Ns or sts in HP on LHS	
K 4 rows	14
These last 12 rows form the pattern	
Continue in pattern to 134 rows (11 patterns)	134
W 8 rows	142
K 2 rows	144

Use cast on row to make a hem over all sts
Cast off over all sts in M, adding matching cotton for strength if you wish. This will form the underarm seamline, so cast off at the correct tension.

Knit another sleeve in the same way

Back and fronts knitted in one piece
	RC
Always put stitches in holding on the LHS of 'right' side of garment.	
Cast on 127 sts in M on 3·25 mm (US size 3)	
Ns or T6	0
W 12 rows	12
Put 17 sts or Ns in HP on LHS	
K 4 rows	16
Bring HP to WP	
W 1 row	17
Inc 1 st on LHS edge on this and next 6 rows,	
W 7 rows	24
Put 24 sts or Ns in HP on LHS	
K 4 rows	28
Bring HP to WP	
W 1 row	29
Cast on 6 sts using M on LHS, W rest of row	30
W 6 rows	36
Put 30 Ns or sts in HP on LHS	
K 4 rows	40
Continue in pattern as before, to 108 rows	108

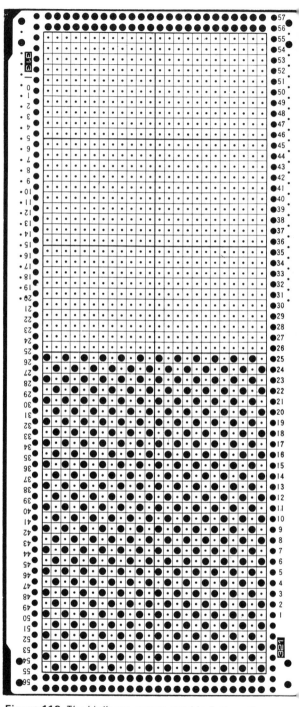

Figure 118 *The bird's eye pattern used in Patterns 2 and 3, showing punched and unpunched sections of a punchcard*

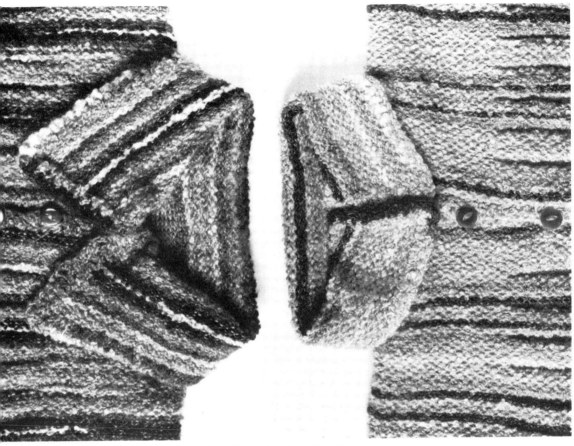

Figure 119 *Two ways to wear the collar of the jacket in Pattern 2*

Knit across all sts	109
Cast off 50 sts in M at LHS, K rest of row	110
K 1 row	111
Cast on 50 sts in M at LHS,	
K 1 row	112
Change to W and pattern as before	
Pattern to 312 rows	312
K 1 row across all sts	313
Cast off 50 sts in M at LHS, K rest of row	314
K 1 row	315
Cast on 50 sts in M at LHS	
K 1 row	316
Continue in pattern to row 388	388
W 6 rows	394
Using a spare piece of M, cast off 6 sts at *end*	
of next row, then W across rest of sts	395
W 1 row	396
Put 24 Ns or sts in HP on LHS	
K 4 rows	400
Bring HP to WP	
W 1 row	401

Dec 1 st on LHS on next 7 rows, W 7 rows	408
Put 17 sts or Ns in HP at LHS	
K 4 rows	412
Bring HP to WP	
W 12 rows	424
Cast off in M over all sts	

Collar

Cast on 90 sts in M on 3·25 mm (US size 3)	
Ns or T6	1
K 1 row	2
W 3 rows	5
Inc 1 st each end of next and every foll 4th row	
to 110 sts	41
W 4 rows	45
Cast off across all sts in M	

The collar could be knitted on if the shoulder seams are seamed first. The shoulders could be shaped by applying the appropriate 'tapering' methods given in Chapter 6.

Figure 120 *Back view of the suit illustrated in plate 6*

adjusting the crochet to take account of the collar corners. Now crochet down the LHS front, make 2 chain to turn, crochet back up this front, round the collar until the RHS collar point is reached. Round the corner, then make a buttonhole by making 2 chain and missing 1 dc st. Crochet 7 dc, and make a further buttonhole. Continue to make buttonholes in this way until you're near the RHS bottom corner. Now continue the line of dc round this corner and along the hemline of the jacket, crocheting over the looped weaving yarn to anchor and hide it. Fasten off when you reach the LHS corner.

Make a line of double crochet round each sleeve cuff, narrowing the cuff if you prefer it that way.

Sew on buttons to correspond to buttonholes.

The collar can be worn buttoned up and turned over – like a roll collar – or open. (See figure 119.)

Alternatively, start and end the front sections with a hemmed st-st band, and slip stitch a hem at cuff and hemline. The collar could be made in M, using the HP and a st-st fabric doubled back on itself.

Permutations

The pink suit jacket in plate 6 (facing p. 96) and figure 120 was knitted to this pattern, with a longer body and hemmed bands to start and finish. The sleeves were set in the other way round, using the wider end to make a different sleeve finish, and making the sleeve wide enough to fit the armhole. Elastic was used to produce ruffles, and the garment was edged in a shell crochet stitch. A different knitweave pattern was used, and a different combination of yarns made quite a different fabric. The tie belt is threaded through the weaving yarn at the waistline.

The silver/grey evening jacket in figure 66 was also knitted to this pattern. Here the combination of a metallic yarn with an acrylic poodle yarn produced a stiffer fabric, and the sleeves were successfully left wide at the cuff. The jacket was made reversible; worn silver side out, it looks glamorous but is very warm. Worn silver side in, there's less glitter and it's more suitable for afternoon wear.

The heavier jacket, shown in plate 7 (facing p. 97) and figure 121 and suitable for both men and women, is another permutation on this style. This has straight, set-in sleeves, and rounded sleeve hemlines. The brown jacket in figure 6 is a variation of Pattern 2.

The length of both sleeves and jacket are easy to adjust; just knit over a greater or lesser number of stitches. A triple knitting yarn used for weaving in the basic jacket pattern, and an open-ended zip

Finishing The shoulder seams are formed by joining the appropriate side edges of the front and back pieces. Seam the shoulders and sew on the collar.

Hold the jacket with the right side facing you. Using a 3·5 mm (US size E/4) hook and A, double crochet up the RHS front and round the collar,

Figure 121 *Back view of the jacket shown in plate 7. The stripes are varied to give added interest*

fastened at the front – with elastic threaded through several rows of knitweave at the waist – would make a good, hard-wearing bomber jacket.

Sideways knitted skirts with mock pleats

Using the holding position with knitweave, or a contrast of heavy and light yarns, is a good way to make a skirt with mock pleats. Figure 102 shows one version. The garment pattern is very simple, though the length is restricted by the number of needles available on a particular knitting machine – hand knitters, of course, can knit to any length they like, provided they can comfortably hold the large numbers of stitches on their needles.

In effect, the pattern is similar to the sleeve pattern for the jacket: the pleated part forms the hemline, the knitwoven part forms the yoke. In order to have a tight-fitting waist, it's useful to use the holding position not only for the pleats, but also to shape the skirt yoke.

A useful pattern would read like this:

Skirt	RC
Cast on 200 sts in M	
W 2 rows across all sts or Ns	2
Put 20 sts or Ns at LHS in HP	
W 4 rows on these 180 sts or Ns	6
Bring HP to WP	
W 2 rows	8
Put 60 sts or Ns at LHS in HP	
K 6 rows	14
Bring HP to WP	

This can be used as a 14 row 'loop' pattern, that is, you simply repeat it from the beginning until you have the correct waist measurement, given by the LHS edge.

To finish the skirt, make a hem with the cast-on row from RHS to LHS, then leave an opening to insert a zip, about 20 cm ($8\frac{1}{2}$ in.) long. I like to back

131

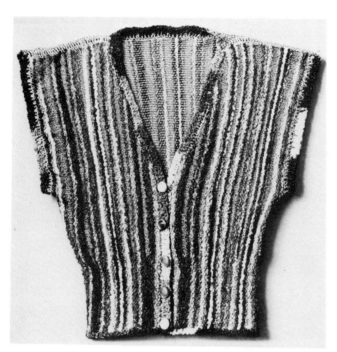

Figure 122 *A sideways knitted waistcoat; Pattern 2 used in a slightly different way*

the waistline of my skirts with a wide elastic fitting precisely to my waist measurement; this gives a neat finish and holds in blouses, as well as stiffening the waist. (See figure 100.)

The hemline can be finished in all kinds of ways; crochet, fringes, hems. For extra length, knit a long panel to fit the hemline, either as it is (to give pattern contrast) or perhaps gathered for a romantic frill.

Ponchos The same technique can be used to make a poncho. This can take a lot of knitting – I made one which took over 800 rows – but the method produces a front-fastening poncho without seams and the shaping method is very versatile.

Waistcoats Another good way to make use of this pattern is to make a sideways knitted waistcoat. This time the woven section will be at the waistline, the wider, pleated section over the bust and forming the sleeve, as shown in figure 122. There are many ways to finish this type of waistcoat; you can leave the sleeves wide and dropped, gather them at the shoulder, cuff or both, vary the neckline, and so on. Match the waistcoat with a skirt knitted on the same principle, and cinch the waist with a cummerbund. You'll have a warm, comfortable and exclusive outfit.

Pattern 3 – The raglan jacket

The pattern is for a basic raglan jacket with a rounded neckline; the garment is knitted in two yarns of different textures in two stitch patterns to give a reversible jacket suitable for men, women and children. The pattern illustrates some of the advantages of knitting from the neck downwards. It's shown in plate 3 (facing p. 73).

Materials 375 gm (13 oz) of a medium (2/14s) Shetland wool was used as M, and 100 gm ($3\frac{1}{2}$ oz) of a 3-ply acrylic bouclé, Saturn from Silverknit, was used as A. The top section feels lighter and softer to the touch, the lower section gives good 'hang' to the garment, and a pleasant fabric contrast. Ten round wooden buttons are used at the edge of the garment, and to finish the cording.

Measurements
Chest 91 cm ($35\frac{3}{4}$ in.)
Underarm seam 37 cm ($14\frac{1}{2}$ in.)
Length from shoulder to waist 38 cm (15 in.)
Length from shoulder to hem 70 cm ($27\frac{1}{2}$ in.)

Stitch patterns *Pattern 1*: The top sections of body and sleeves are knitted in a simple bird's eye fairisle pattern, using chart 2 from Pattern 2. It's the difference in texture rather than colour which produces the fabric.
Pattern 2: The lower sections of the body and sleeves are worked in doubled yarn knitted in st-st on large size Ns or on every other N on the machine. For hand knitting, knit 2 sts together across the first pattern row. For machine knitting, transfer every other st to its adjacent needle, pushing the empty Ns back to the NWP.

Tension The garment was knitted on a punchcard machine. T8 produced a tension of 28 sts and 32 rows over 10 cm (4 in.) for the fairisle, and T10 produced a tension of 17 sts and 28 rows over 10 cm (4 in.) with the yarn doubled and used on every other needle. Hand knitters should find 3·5 mm Ns (US size 4) suitable for the fairisle and 5 mm Ns (US size 7) suitable for the doubled st-st fabric.

The main garment pieces are worked downwards. Using the quickest increasing method on the machine – that is simply bringing a new needle into the WP at the beginning of the relevant rows – makes it easy to do the raglan shaping.

132

Jacket

Sleeve

	RC
Cast on 21 sts in M using T8 or 3·5 mm (US size 4) Ns	1
K in pattern 1	
Inc 1 st at beg of *every* row to 101 sts	81
Cast on 3 sts at the beg of the next 2 rows (107 sts)	83
K in pattern 1 for 28 rows (adjust length here)	111
Prepare for pattern 2, using 5 mm (US size 7) Ns or T10 (54 sts)	
K in pattern 2 for 80 rows	191
Cast off *loosely* over all sts	

Knit a second sleeve in the same way

Back

Cast on 41 sts in M using 3·5 mm Ns (US size 4) or T8	1
K in pattern 1	
Inc 1 st at beg of every row to 121 sts	81
Cast on 3 sts at beg of next 2 rows (127 sts)	83
K 28 rows (adjust length here)	111
Prepare for pattern 2, using 5 mm Ns (US size 7) or T10 (64 sts)	
K 9 rows in pattern 2	120
Inc 1 st each side of next and every foll 10th row to 181 rows (78 sts)	181
K 20 rows	201
Cast off *loosely*	

Fronts

Knit the first front, shaping at the LHS

Cast on 22 sts in M, using 3·5 mm (US size 4) Ns or T8	1
K in pattern 1	
Put all except the first 2 sts on LHS in HP	
Inc 1 st on LHS and k 1 row	2
K 1 row	3
Inc 1 st on LHS and bring 1 st or N from HP to WP and k 1 row	4
K 1 row	5
Repeat these 2 rows 6 times	17
Inc 1 st on LHS and bring rem 13 sts or Ns from HP to WP and k 1 row	18
K 1 row	19
Continue inc 1 st on LHS *only* until there are 62 sts	80
K 1 row	81
Cast on 3 sts on LHS and k 1 row (65 sts)	82
K for 28 rows (adjust length here)	110
K 1 row	111

Prepare for pattern 2 (33 sts)	
K in pattern 2. K 9 rows	120
Inc 1 st on LHS on next and every foll 10th row to 181 rows (40 sts)	181
K 20 rows	201
Cast off *loosely*	

Knit the second front, reversing the shaping.

Collar

The collar is knitted in pattern 2

Cast on 61 sts in doubled yarn on 5 mm Ns (US size 7) or T10	1
K 2 rows	3
Put 1 st at *beg* of each row in HP for next 14 rows	17
Bring 1 st from HP to WP at *beg* of each of next 14 rows	31
K 2 rows	33
Make a hem with the cast on sts	
Cast off over all sts.	

The collar can be knitted onto the garment if the raglans are seamed before starting the collar.

Finishing Seam the raglan edges. The latch-up method is quick, simple and reversible; use the large loops of the increased stitches. Sew the side and sleeve seam in a reversible stitch. Sew the longer edge of the collar to the neckline in a reversible seam. With a 3·5 mm (US size E/4) crochet hook, and using the two yarns doubled, work one row of double crochet round the sleeve cuffs.

Hold the garment with the stocking stitch side facing you. Starting at the LHS front, make a row of half treble crochet down this front. Continue along the hemline, using a double crochet stitch. Change to a half treble stitch when you reach the RHS front, crochet up the front and finish at the neckline. Sew in the yarn end.

Make two cords of chain crochet, using doubled yarn and the 3·5 mm (US size E/4) hook. Thread these through the neckline and through the holes at the waistline made by knitting two stitches together. Sew buttons to the ends of the cords, and at the edge of the crochet bands, as shown in the illustration. The spaces between the treble crochet stitches can be used as buttonholes, and the garment can be worn either using the st-st side or the purl side as the right side.

Permutations

This garment gives the basic raglan shaping; it's very easy to adapt for a raglan sweater or even a dress. Knit one front neck shaping, put these stitches on a spare needle or in the HP; then knit the second front shaping. Now bring all the stitches to the knitting position or onto the same needle, and continue as for the back.

Increasing the raglan by 1 st at the beginning of every row is satisfactory for most medium yarns and their tensions. For bulky or fine yarns, or for special patterns such as tuck or slip stitch, you may have to adjust the number of rows between the increases. Just work out a smooth increase between the smallest and largest number of stitches needed, over the number of rows needed, as explained in the section on tapering in Chapter 6.

The same pattern can be used to knit zip-fronted shirts, tuck stitch T-shirts (as in plate 8, facing p. 97) – where the front and the back can be knitted quite simply without any neck shaping – and even for dresses by continuing to increase after the hip has been reached until you have the length you want from waist to hem. Don't forget to finish by making a curved hemline, as discussed in Chapter 6. Additional fullness can be added to skirts by introducing a tuck stitch or knitweave pattern in the lower section of the skirts; waists can be shaped by knitting the body sections in a rib stitch and varying the tension. Sleeves can be tapered to narrower or wider shapes, the body can be knitted straight or shaped. The neckline can be varied, the raglan seamline emphasised by joining with set-in crochet lace or other devices, possibly in a different colour from the main garment.

If you start at the waist, preferably with a hem to thread wide elastic through, and knit a tapered piece downwards, finishing with a curved hemline, you have a skirt panel. Make two for a skirt like the one in plate 6 (facing p. 96).

Pattern 4 – The fitted sweater

I've written up a pattern for the ubiquitous fitted sweater because it is, after all, the knitwear most people want most of the time. It does take a little more skill than the basic sweater using the rectangles – in particular, the neck shaping takes a little practice. Very old knitting machines, where the yarn is simply laid over the needles, are easier for this type of shaping; you can knit the left and right sides at the same time, by using two separate balls of yarn. The same is true of hand knitting. You're assured of getting both sides the same, with or without mistakes!

The pattern is for a round-necked sweater knitted in a two-tone all-over fairisle and illustrated in plate 4 (facing p. 73). The shape is very popular with men, in this or a V-necked form, and is also a favourite with children. The sleeveless version, at one time considered purely a man's garment, is now part of most people's wardrobe.

Materials 375 gm (13 oz) of Falcon's 4-ply Superwash wool in M and 250 gm ($8\frac{1}{2}$ oz) of Falcon's 4-ply Superwash in A. Though the amounts will vary slightly with the particular fairisle pattern used, what really matters is which yarn you use for welts and background and which for the fill-in pattern.

Measurements
Chest 115 cm ($45\frac{1}{4}$ in.)
Length from shoulder 74 cm (29 in.)
Underarm seam 56 cm (22 in.)
Cuff 9·5 cm ($3\frac{3}{4}$ in.)
Armhole 25 cm (10 in.).

Stitch pattern The main body was knitted in 2-colour stocking stitch, the welts, cuffs and neckband in 1×1 rib in M. the 24 st repeat pattern is given in chart 3 (figure 123), adapted from Knitmaster basic card 16 by elongating the pattern on some rows. Row by row instructions are outside the scope of this book, so hand knitters will have to consider how to place the pattern symmetrically on each garment piece. The punchcard will deal with this automatically if it's properly aligned with the needles.

Tension The garment was knitted on a punchcard machine fitted with a ribber. T10 produced a tension of 28 sts and 32 rows to 10 cm (4 in.), measured over the fairisle pattern. The ribbing was knitted at T3/4. Hand knitters should find 4 mm Ns (US size 5) satisfactory for the fairisle, and 3 mm Ns (US size 2) for the ribbing.

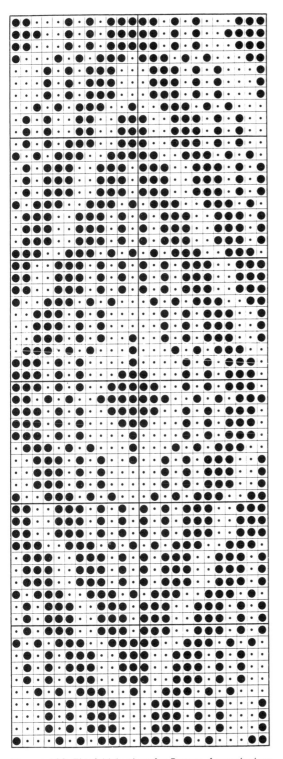

Figure 123 *The fairisle chart for Pattern 4 punched on a 24-space punchcard*

Sweater

Consider how to centre the pattern before starting to knit each piece

Back	RC
*Cast on 161 sts in M for 1×1 rib K at T3/4	1
or on 3 mm Ns (US size 2) for 39 rows	40
Change to T10 or 4 mm Ns (US size 5) and	
pattern knitting	
K in pattern for 120 rows	160
Cast off 7 sts at the end of the next 2 rows,	
using spare yarn	162
Dec 1 st at end of next 20 rows (127 sts)**	182
K for 61 rows	243
Put all sts on a holder or spare needle, or strip	
off with waste yarn	

Front	
K as for back to row 182 (* to **)	182
K straight for 33 rows (Pattern row 55)	215
Keep 19 sts at centre on a st holder or spare	
yarn	
Work on RHS 54 sts, putting LHS 54 sts in HP	
Dec 1 st at neck edge on the next 12 rows	
(42 sts)	227
K for 16 rows	243
Put these 42 sts on holder or spare needle, or	
strip off with waste yarn.	

Bring 54 sts on LHS into WP
Reset card to Pattern 55, RC to 215
Work LHS like RHS reversing shaping
Put 42 sts on holder or spare needle.

Sleeve	
	RC
Cast on 85 sts in M, using 3 mm Ns (US size	
2) or KM	
K on T3/4 or 3 mm Ns (US size 2) for 34 rows	35
Change to 4 mm Ns (US size 5) or T10 and	
pattern knitting	
K 10 rows	45
Inc 1 st each end of next and every foll 6th row	
to 123 sts	154
K 10 rows	164
Cast off 7 sts at the end of the next 2 rows,	
using spare yarn	166
Dec 1 st at the end of the next 12 rows	178
Dec 1 st at *both* ends on the next 29 rows	206
Cast off remaining sts, or thread them on	
spare yarn.	

Finishing Combine the shoulder stitches from the back and fronts, and cast them off together as described in Chapter 8.

Sew the sleeve head into the armholes. Sew the side and sleeve underarm seams.

Neckband Holding the 'right' side of the fabric towards you and using 3 mm (US size 2) twin pins, slip 19 centre front sts on the pins, pick up 28 sts along the left neck edge, slip 43 sts from centre back on the pins, pick up 28 sts along the right neck edge. K on these sts in 1 × 1 rib for 12 rows. Cast off in rib.

Permutations

The permutations on this particular theme are of course well known. The first, and perhaps the simplest, is to knit the sweater body without the sleeves – a slipover. Make the armholes a little longer, perhaps 2 or 3 cm (1 or 1¼ in.) and compensate for this by shortening the length from welt to armhole; this will give quite sufficient space to fit an armhole band.

Vary the sleeves to vary the sweater; use cap sleeves, short, puffed, three quarter, wide, narrow, rectangular . . . the choice is yours.

Divide the front into a right and left hand side, and you have a cardigan. Different ways of tackling the bands have already been discussed, and adding patch pockets again increases the permutations without the need for new skills.

Take away the sleeves, and you have a waistcoat. Figure 103 shows a little tuck stitch one, with fronts shaped by using the holding position and the edgings all done in crochet. You can easily make a reversible garment in this way; done in a glitter yarn, it's a most helpful evening accessory, popular for both men and women.

There's no need to stop at the waistline for this sweater: turn it into a dress by adding length and by increasing the width with side shaping and careful selection of stitch patterns. Let yourself go with colours as well as patterns; vary the length with the fashion.

This type of garment can be knitted from side to side just as easily as any of the others, and this will not only increase the pattern range, it will make the neck shaping easier. The snag here is that welts, unless they're plain hems, have to be knitted and attached separately. They can, of course, be knitted on.

Enlarge the dimensions, and the pattern will do very nicely for jackets, coats and even sleeping-bags for the baby.

So now you've seen what *can* readily be done. Now, knowing this, let your own ideas 'materialise', take on the shape, the form, which you'd only had in mind before. Don't worry about experts; just start to knit in your own, individual way. Don't mind mistakes; welcome them as steps, perhaps, to something just as useful as – and maybe more exciting than – the garment that you started out to make. Get to know the simple tools, explore the possibilities of the machines, enjoy the feel and colour of the raw materials. Then have the confidence, the faith, to turn even the plainest yarns into the finest and most creative forms of knitted craft.

KNITTING MACHINE DISTRIBUTORS AND YARN SUPPLIERS

United Kingdom knitting machine manufacturers and importers

Brother Machines
Jones Sewing Machine Company Ltd
Sheply Street
Guide Bridge
Audenshaw
Manchester M34 5JD
Telephone: 061 330 6531

J+B House
869 High Road
Finchley
London N12 8QW
Telephone: 01 446 3231

Knitmaster Machines
Knitmaster Ltd
30–40 Elcho Street
London SW11 4AX
Telephone: 01 228 9303

Passap Machines
Bogod Machine Company Ltd
50–52 Great Sutton Street
London EC1
Telephone: 01 253 1198

Singer Machines
The Singer Company (UK) Ltd
255 High Street
Guildford
Surrey GU1 3DH
Telephone: 0483 71144

Superba Machines
Barry Bryant Ltd
Walk Mills
The Walk
Coney Lane
Keighley
West Yorkshire
Telephone: 0535 65266 & 604588

Toyota Machines
Aisin (UK) Ltd
34 High Street
Bromley
Kent
Telephone: 01 460 8866

United Kingdom yarn suppliers

Cone Knit Spinning (Bradford)
32 Rebecca Street
Bradford BD1 2RY

A good range of machine knitting yarns on cones, including 2-ply Orlon. Overseas orders taken.

Hilary Chetwynd,
Kipping Cottage
Cheriton
Alresford
Hampshire

Specialist in natural coloured silks. Personal service, with advice given. Prefers small orders under 4·5 kg (10 lb) unless asked to import a special order. Overseas orders taken.

Derwent Fabrics
58 Main Street
Keswick
Cumbria CA12 5JS

Jacob, Black Welsh, oiled Aran, Swaledale and Herdwick hand knitting wools. These are all supplied undyed and the right thickness for Aran patterns. Overseas orders taken.

R S Duncan and Co
Falcon Mills,
Bargle Lane
Bradford
West Yorkshire BD7 4QJ

A large range of knitting yarns, mostly in 20, 25 or 50 gm balls, a few 'pull balls' and cones. A good variety of mixed fibre yarns. Chlorofibre. Overseas orders taken.

Foster Textile Sales Ltd
88/96 Market Street West
Preston
Lancashire PR1 2HR

Machine knitting yarns on cones at competitive prices. The range includes machine washable pure new wool.

The Greenwood Spinning Company Ltd
PO Box 4
Victoria Mills
Heckmondwike
West Yorkshire WF16 ODG

A selection of knitting yarns in 20 and 25 gm balls, and some 4-ply on 250 gm cones. 3-ply crochet cotton, 'fleck' yarns, marls and random knittings.

William Hall and Co (Monsall) Ltd
177 Stanley Road
Cheadle Hulme
Cheadle
Cheshire SK8 6RF

An outstanding range of knitting and weaving yarns, including linen hand weaving yarns from Sweden, brushed lustre wool, undyed and space dyed, large range of chenille wools and other yarns, cotton and viscose fancy from extremely fine to bulky, mostly undyed. Supplied on cones. Overseas orders taken.

Hermit Wools Ltd
Airedale Mills
Ives Street
Shipley
West Yorkshire BD17 7EL

Good range of ordinary weight and chunky knitting wools, supplied in 20, 25 and 50 gm balls. Fleck, marl and random dyed yarns.

Holmfirth Wools
Briggate
Windhill
Shipley
Yorkshire BD18 2BS

Excellent range of Woolmarked DK, 3- and 4-ply machine washable wool available on cone or in 25 gm balls. 2-ply wool on cones. A further range of balled yarns in wool, synthetics and cotton. Overseas orders taken.

Holywell Textile Mills Ltd
Holywell
North Wales CH8 7NU

Undyed Jacob sheep wool, supplied in 50 gm balls, in hank or on cone, scoured or in oil.

T. M. Hunter Ltd
Sutherland Wool Mills
Brora
Scotland KW9 6NA

A good range of Scottish wools. Minimum order is for 4·5 kg (10 lbs) in a variety of shades and qualities. Overseas orders taken.

Jamieson & Smith Ltd
90 North Road
Lerwick
Shetland Isles ZE1 0PQ

Very large range of dyed Shetland wools ranging from 2-ply lace weight to heavy 3-ply Embo yarns. The colours are exceptionally beautiful; some wools are supplied on cone, all can be had in 6 gm (2 oz) hanks. Overseas orders taken.

Mailyarns Ltd
38 High Street
Syston
Leicester

A range of unusual yarns, including glitter threads, invisible nylon, 100% acrylic fine ply and 100% knitting cotton on cones. Nylostrip for rug and carpet knitting.

Silverknit
The Old Mill
Epperstone By-Pass
Woodborough
Nottingham NG14 6DH

A very good range of fine yarns on 200 gm cones. The range of colours is particularly good, and the fibres range from pure wool, cotton and viscose to mixtures including Alpaca, Angora, Lambswool, acrylic fibres and brushed mohair yarns. There is also a good range of 'Silverknit' glitter yarns, and toning 30's cotton for punch lace knitting, as well as gold and silver threads and invisible nylon. The range is not cheap, but it is very useful for original design work. Overseas orders taken.

Yorkshire Wool Company
6 Spring Gardens
Bradford BD1 3EL

A good range of coned knitting yarns, including 2-ply Orlon. A greater range of 20, 25 and 50 gm balled yarns and random dyed yarns in double knitting wool, 4-ply triacetate and nylon, and spot prints in acrylic and nylon. Overseas orders taken.

United States knitting machine manufacturers, importers and distributors

Brother Machines
Brother International Corporation
900 Lunt Avenue
Elk Grove Village
Illinois 60007
Telephone: (800) 323–0592

Passap and Superba Knitting Machines
555 5th Avenue
New York
New York 10017
Telephone: (212) 867–6181

Studio Machines
Studio Yarn Farms Inc
10002 14th Avenue, SW
PO Box 46017
Seattle
Washington 98146
Telephone: (206) 763–1310

Toyota Machines
Newton Knits
9836 Garden Grove Boulevard
Garden Grove
California 92600
Telephone: (714) 530–6551

United States yarn suppliers

Bare Hill Studios
East Bare Hill Road
Harvard
Massachusetts 01451
Telephone: (617) 456–8669

Sample cards sent for $1. Yarns made of all kinds of fibres sold on cones or in skeins. Large quantity mill ends supplied at very competitive prices.

Colonial Woollen Mills Inc
5611 Hughs Avenue
Cleveland
Ohio 44100
Telephone: (216) 391–0234

Sample cards sent. Specialises in acrylics but also handles some wools.

Fibre Yarn Co
840 Sixth Avenue
New York
New York 10001
Telephone: (212) 683–0731

A wide assortment of yarns in a large range of colours available. Does not send samples.

Knitcraft Distributors (Marjorie Bandlow)
10301 Truman Road
Independence
Missouri 64052
Telephone: (816) 461–1248

Main distributor of yarns for Brother machines.

Landau Yarns Inc
7 East Garden Place
Pompton Plains
New Jersey 07444
Telephone: (201) 835–9343

Huge selection of every kind of yarn, made of natural and man-made fibres. Large selection of colours. Deals wholesale and retail. Sends sample cards. Deals in first quality yarns from all over the world, and gives good prices on large orders.

Mary Maxim Inc
2001 Holland Avenue
Port Huron
Michigan 48060
Telephone: (313) 987–2000

Sample cards for $1. Handles all types of yarns.

The Niddy Noddy
416 Albany Post Road
Croton-on-Hudson
New York 10520

Will send sample cards. Specialises in fancy yarns. Hand dyes cottons, wools, mohairs, silks and rayons in a large range of colours.

Quicknit
231 East 53 Street
New York
New York 10022

Specialises in natural fibres; wools, cottons, silks, angora, bouclés, mohair. Has some hand dyed and handspun yarns. Offers approximately 300 colours, but does not send samples. High fashion colours a feature.

School Products Co Inc
1201 Broadway
New York,
New York 10001
Telephone (212) 679–3516

Sends sample cards. Specialises in wool and some fancy yarns in approximately 150 shades.

FURTHER READING LIST

Abbey, Barbara, *Knitting Lace*, Pitman Publishing, 1974

Anthony, Jane, *Machine Knitting – A Practical Guide*, Macdonald and Jane's, 1977

The Batsford Book of Knitting and Crochet, ed Thelma M Nye, Batsford, 1973

The Complete Book of Knitting, Crochet and Embroidery, ed Pam Dawson, Marshall Cavendish Ltd, 1976

Gartshore, Linda, *The Craft of Machine Knitting*, Stanley Paul, 1978

Holbourne, David, *The Book of Machine Knitting*, Batsford, 1979

Kinder, Kathleen, *A Resource Book for Machine Knitters*, Kathleen Kinder (Valley View, Station Road, Giggleswick, Settle, North Yorkshire BD24 0AB), 1979

Lorant, Tessa, *Earning and Saving with a Knitting Machine*, Book 1 in *Profitable Knitting Series*, The Thorn Press, The Old Vicarage, Godney, Wells, Somerset, 1980

Thomas, Mary, *Mary Thomas's Book of Knitting Patterns*, Hodder and Stoughton Ltd, 6th impression, 1968

Thomas, Mary, *Mary Thomas's Knitting Book*, Dover reprint, 1972

Weaver, Mary, *The Ribbing Attachment*, Weaverknits Ltd, (276–278 Main Road Sutton-at-Hone, Near Dartford, Kent) Part I 1974, Part II 1976

Machine knitting publications

Worldwide Machine Knitting (monthly magazine from newsagents or by subscription)
Stitch in Time – Jones and Brother publication
Passap Model Books – Passap International publication
Pattern Libraries for punchcard knitters – Knitmaster, Jones and Brother

INDEX